As a therapist who uses photographs ther..., couple therapy, I strongly recommend this book to any clinician who is ..... in Phototherapy and Therapeutic Photography.

I represent the Instituto de la Familia. IFAC (México). This year we are celebrating 50 years training family and couples therapists. For more than 15 years the subject of phototherapy and therapeutic photography has been taught in our institute, for which we welcome the forthcoming appearance of this Del Loewenthal handbook, because its content will be very useful for our purposes.

Dr. Francisco Avilés, *Gutiérrez, Head of Teaching,*
Instituto de la familia IFAC

Professor Loewenthal draws together the various ways in which photography can be used across disciplines in this timely publication. Using examples from his own personal and professional experiences he provides essential guidance for anyone looking to incorporate photography into their own practice. This is a welcome addition to the growing evidence base to support these techniques.

Dr Neil Gibson, *Robert Gordon University, Aberdeen: Author of Therapeutic*
Photography: Enhancing Self-Esteem, Self-Efficacy and Resilience

I very much welcome Del Loewenthal´s Handbook of Phototherapy and Therapeutic Photography for therapists and clients. Del Loewenthal is an excellent professional as a psychotherapist as well as a photographer. His book includes theories, case studies and exercises on existing and new approaches together with chapters on such important overarching aspects as ethics, training and research. It can be seen that he understands very well what it means to use photographs in therapy in our digital age. I warmly recommend his book to anyone who is interested in new approaches to psychotherapy and therapeutic work.

Ulla Halkola, *Mssc, psychotherapist, phototherapy trainer and photo artist.*
Honorary Member of the Finnish Phototherapy Association

This rich, engaging and substantial handbook introduces all the major approaches and basic techniques of Phototherapy and Therapeutic Photography. It combines theory, methods, techniques along with case studies, and provides an excellent resource for therapists, other professionals, clients, researchers and trainers. As a valuable aid to self-development it addresses also self-help for the client and activist client.

Philia Issari, *is Professor of Counselling Psychology and Director of the*
Laboratory of Qualitative Research in Psychology and Psychosocial Well-Being,
in the department of Psychology at National and Kapodistrian University of
Athens. She is co-author of the book "Visual & Arts-based Qualitative
Research Methods (in Gr.) (Open Academic Editions, 2022)

This book brings together a thoughtful compilation of materials that expand the spectrum of practitioners' tools to embrace digital means, in particular, digital photography, that has become such a prevalent part of our culture. In each chapter, poignant vignettes and case examples richly illuminate the potential of phototherapy and therapeutic photography so that approaches can be readily understood by readers. Upon completion of this book, readers will have a deeper understanding of how photographic discourse and strategies may enhance and support clients' well-being by keeping abreast of changes in our cultural practices and technologies.

Alexander Kopytin, *Professor, Psychology Department, St.-Petersburg Academy of Post-Graduate Pedagogica Education*

The Handbook of Phototherapy and Therapeutic Photography is essential reading for anyone with an interest in the transformative potential of photography. It will be useful for psychotherapists, psychoanalysts, counsellors, and others wanting to explore strategies of personal growth, self-help, and self-discovery. There is a detailed engagement with therapeutic visual approaches, including photo-cards, re-enactment phototherapy, and portraiture. Drawing on carefully selected case studies, the book illustrates how photography supports and extends conventional talking therapies by ethically enabling participants to articulate their thoughts, feelings, and emotions.

Dr Dawn Mannay, *Author - Visual, Narrative, and Creative Research Methods: Application, Reflection and Ethics* (Routledge)

The Handbook of Phototherapy and Therapeutic Photography comprehensively captures the multifaceted nature of photography as a tool for therapy, coaching, activism, and research. Addressed to a wide audience of psychological and art therapists, researchers, and clients themselves, Del Lowenthal's book zooms in on the often-understated potential of images in the process of healing and personal development, through a selection of insightful case studies, techniques, and practical exercises. In an era marked by digital technology, this compendium brings the universal language of photography as a form of expression and inclusion, and foundation for therapeutic communication, to the next level.

Dr Lucian Milasan, *Researcher and Lecturer in Mental Health, Nottingham Trent University*

The experience of reading The Handbook is like that of travelling to a country, "Photo-Therapy Land", guided by a sophisticate cicerone, Del Loewenthal, and visiting the most prominent towns, that's to say the five major approaches to using photography, as a visual medium, therapeutically.

The group of travellers, composed by therapists, photographers, other professionals, clients, and self-help activists, are accompanied into a variety of scenarios, through insightful case studies, accurate explanations and stimulating exercises.

Coming back from the journey, it remains the desire to return to "Photo-Therapy Land" one day, to find out new itineraries, discover hidden little villages and explore invisible landscapes far beyond the bridge of verbal communication.

Ayres Marques Pinto, *Coordinator of GRIFO – Gruppo di Ricerca Internazionale sulla Foto-Terapia and International Photo-Therapy Research Group*

Phototherapy and Therapeutic Photography have a long history but never have they been more relevant and important than in today's complex world. Del Loewenthal is one of the leading academics in the field and is well-placed to explore how they are used by practitioners across a wide-range of real-world settings. His book brings together current research, provides new insights through real-world examples, and offers practical exercises in how phototherapy and therapeutic photography can be applied. It is highly recommended.

Dr Michael Pritchard, *Director of Programmes, The Royal Photographic Society*

Can photographs bring about therapeutic change? This remarkable handbook sets out to illuminate the many ways that phototherapy and therapeutic photography can help to release feelings into words, facilitating psychological development. Written for both clients and practitioners, Del Loewenthal, a master-practitioner in the field, provides us with a feast of fascinating ideas from individual and organisational case studies to issues concerning theoretical approaches, techniques, research methods and professional training.

For those seeking creative inspiration and new avenues for personal growth, I cannot recommend this book too highly.

Rosemary Rizq, *Professor of Psychoanalytic Psychotherapy, University of Roehampton*

Photography officially became a therapeutic tool of the psychotherapy and counseling field; photography brings into the therapeutic relationship the dimension of the 'here and now', it allows to perceive the own individual life history and its new elaboration. The book written by Prof. Del helps to clarify the phototherapeutic intervention and its methodology through theoretical framework and the support of clinical cases.

Oliviero Rossi, *Psychologist-Psychotherapist Director of the Expressive Gestalt Psychotherapy Institute, Rome. Former Director: Methods of the image in the relationship of help, Pontifical Antonianum University, Rome*

Photographs and photographing can be used as stimuli to relive and recall experiences and memories, and to express emotions, promoting the person's self-understanding, moreover they compensate for communication problems.

Despite this consideration, only a few studies have investigated the role of images in clinical practice.

Starting from the idea that the human mind does not function using only a verbal code, this amazing and revelatory book provides theories and examples of how photographs and photographing may activate a different and more immediate language, with a stronger symbolic and emotional value, and thus promote personal and clinical improvement.

Emanuela Saita, *Psychologist, PhD, Full Professor at the Faculty of Psychology of Catholic University of Sacred Heart (Milan, Italy)*

It is rare to find a psychotherapist who is both an accomplished photographer and someone able to explore the multi-layered relationships between the two practices in a way that is guaranteed to generate creativity. From phototherapy and therapeutic photography to portraiture, Del Loewenthal opens up the range of photography's therapeutic uses and potentials, which have never been greater than in this digital age. The handbook, enriched with case material, will be the go-to source for self-help activists, therapeutic practitioners and related professionals of all theoretical orientations, who are interested in developing and refining their work in this burgeoning field.

Robert Snell, *is an analytic and existential psychotherapist in private practice. Author of 'Cézanne and the Post-Bionian Field: An exploration and a meditation'*

Re-think what can be done with a smartphone (or other) camera. When needed words come up short in therapy, pictures or picture-taking can assist in transformative meaning-making. Del Loewenthal engagingly shares his explorations of phototherapy's possibilities, offering useful insights and recommendations for therapists and clients regarding the helping potentials of pictures and picture-taking - in therapy and well beyond.

Prof. Tom Strong, *(Emeritus), University of Calgary. Co-editor The Routledge Handbook of Postmodern Therapies*

In this unique and illuminating work, Del Loewenthal once again regales us with his uncanny ability to challenge our assumptions with a fascinating "look" into the world of photography and its unexpected relevance to psychotherapy, therapeutic photography, and the all too neglected visual medium of our most intimate experiences, feelings, and thoughts about life and now-ubiquitous social medium platforms. This book is bound to become a classic.

M. Guy Thompson, *Ph.D., Founder and Director, New School for Existential Psychoanalysis, author, 'The Death of Desire: An Existential Study in Sanity and Madness'; 'The Legacy of R. D. Laing: An Appraisal of his Contemporary Relevance', both published by Routledge*

Deliberately aimed a wide audience – of not only therapists, but also clients and self-help activists – this book provides both an overview of phototherapy and therapeutic photography as well as detailed accounts of its practice. Beautifully studies, this well-designed book takes the reader through the history of this form of therapy and its various applications, to its use in professional and personal development, action planning, and training. Also, in its discussion of perceptions, subject and object, and ethics, as well as the author's own story, there is a subtle but distinct and powerful political thread to this book – I recommend it highly.

Professor Keith Tudor, *Auckland University of Technology*

Del Loewenthal is in the vanguard of a third wave of phototherapy and therapeutic photography theory and practice. Del turns a fresh lens on the engagement of photography in processes of change and recovery.

Loewenthal's work manifests the circularity of evolving theory and practice.

Del Loewenthal applies praxis to life. This book includes personal case studies from Del's family history alongside case studies from clinical and supervisory practice. As a consummate educator, Loewenthal presents each chapter as like a good seminar, tutorial or supervision session.

Mark Wheeler, is a photographer & UK Phototherapy pioneer working over 35 years in the NHS & third sector as Principal Art Psychotherapist delivering photo-art-therapy & holds a Fellowship of the Royal Photographic Society

The Handbook of Phototherapy and Therapeutic Photography brings together, in one comprehensive and hugely engaging book, the vast knowledge, experience and passion for therapeutic uses of photography by Del Loewenthal, Emeritus Professor of Counselling and Psychotherapy and an internationally renowned author.

A key strength of this book is Prof Loewenthal's ability to draw on many years of personal and professional experience of using, and writing about, Phototheraphy as a tool to explore a vast range of therapeutic applications.

From working with reenactment phototherapy, to therapeutic diaries, to using photo-cards and archival images to unlock hidden narratives, this book is a real tour de force in covering the ever expanding range of possible approaches. In addition to offering exercises and opportunities for experiential learning, the book also provides a historical and theoretical context, discusses ethics and research opportunities.

It will be a go to resource for anyone interested in exploring this exciting and expanding area of practice.

Dr. Julia Winckler, *Principal Lecturer in Photography and Visual Culture, School of Art and Media, University of Brighton*

The Handbook of Phototherapy and Therapeutic Photography

This text introduces the concepts, essential tenets, and basic techniques of phototherapy and therapeutic photography.

Through the use of case studies and the author's own professional experience, this book covers the practices, theories, and research behind phototherapy and therapeutic photography, providing a comprehensive range of major approaches. Examples include Talking Pictures Therapy; re-enactment phototherapy; the creation of therapeutic Photobooks, stories, and diaries; and the therapeutic use of portraiture. Chapters also explain how we can effectively use these techniques in a variety of contexts, including private practice, voluntary organisations, schools, prisons, and management consultancy, as useful adjuncts to primary practices as well as for self-help.

This handbook is for therapists, photographers, other professionals, clients, and activist clients.

Del Loewenthal, PhD is an existential-analytic psychotherapist, photographer, and chartered psychologist. He is a Fellow of the Royal Photographic Society, the British Psychological Society, and the United Kingdom Council for Psychotherapy, and is Emeritus Professor of Psychotherapy and Counselling at the University of Roehampton.

The Handbook of Phototherapy and Therapeutic Photography

For the Professional and Activist Client

Del Loewenthal

Routledge
Taylor & Francis Group

LONDON AND NEW YORK

Designed cover image: Del Loewenthal

First published 2023
by Routledge
4 Park Square, Milton Park, Abingdon, Oxon OX14 4RN

and by Routledge
605 Third Avenue, New York, NY 10158

Routledge is an imprint of the Taylor & Francis Group, an informa business

© 2023 Del Loewenthal

The right of Del Loewenthal to be identified as authorof this work has been asserted in accordance with sections 77 and 78 of the Copyright, Designs and Patents Act 1988.

British Library Cataloguing-in-Publication Data
A catalogue record for this book is available from the British Library

ISBN: 978-1-032-14752-9 (hbk)
ISBN: 978-1-032-14751-2 (pbk)
ISBN: 978-1-003-24091-4 (ebk)

DOI: 10.4324/9781003240914

Typeset in Bembo
by Apex CoVantage, LLC

Contents

Illustrations

Figures

Photographs

Permissions

Extracts from the following are reproduced with the kind permission of the publishers:

Loewenthal, D. (2013a). Talking Pictures Therapy as brief therapy in a school setting. *Journal of Creativity in Mental Health*, 8: 21–34.

Loewenthal, D. (2015). The therapeutic use of photographs in the United Kingdom criminal justice system. *European Journal for Psychotherapy and Counselling*, 17(1): 39–56.

Loewenthal, D. (2020). The therapeutic use of photography: Phototherapy and therapeutic photography. In L. Pauwels and D. Mannay (eds.), *Sage Handbook of Visual Research Methods*, 2nd edition. London: Sage.

Tudor, K., Bettman, C., Bloch-Atefi, A., Day, E., His, T., Loewenthal, D., Low, P. K., O'Neill, G., and van Deurzen, E. (2021). Psychotherapy practice, education, and training during the coronavirus pandemic: Members of the editorial board of the Psychotherapy and Counselling Journal of Australia share their experiences. *Psychotherapy and Counselling Journal of Australia*, 9(1). https://pacja.org.au/2021/04/psychotherapy-practice-education-and-training-during-the-coronavirus-pandemic-members-of-the-editorial-board-of-the-psychotherapy-and-counselling-journal-of-australia-share-their-experiences-2/.

Photograph credits

Cover: Loewenthal

Photo 1.1	Loewenthal
Photo 2.1	Loewenthal
Photo 2.2	Halkola
Photo 3.1	Loewenthal
Photo 3.2	Loewenthal
Photo 3.3	Loewenthal
Photo 3.4	Loewenthal
Photo 3.5	Loewenthal
Photo 3.6	Loewenthal

Photo 3.7   Loewenthal
Photo 4.1   Loewenthal
Photo 5.1   Loewenthal
Photo 5.2   Loewenthal
Photo 5.3   Loewenthal
Photo 5.4   Loewenthal
Photo 5.5   Loewenthal
Photo 5.6   Loewenthal
Photo 5.7   Loewenthal
Photo 5.8   Loewenthal
Photo 5.9   Loewenthal
Photo 5.10   Loewenthal
Photo 5.11   Loewenthal
Photo 5.12   Loewenthal
Photo 5.13   Loewenthal
Photo 6.1   Loewenthal
Photo 6.2   Loewenthal
Photo 7.1   Halkola
Photo 9.1   Loewenthal
Photo 9.2   Loewenthal
Photo 9.3   Loewenthal
Photo 11.1   Halkola
Photo 11.2   Halkola
Photo 12.1   Loewenthal

The author

Del Loewenthal is Fellow of the Royal Photographic Society (FRPS), the British Psychological Society (FBPsS), and the United Kingdom Council for Psychotherapy (UKCPF); he is also Principal Fellow of the Higher Education Authority (PFHEA). He is Emeritus Professor of Psychotherapy and Counselling at the University of Roehampton, UK, and Chair of the Southern Association for Psychotherapy and Counselling (SAFPAC), UK. Del has lectured and conducted workshops on phototherapy and therapeutic photography in Africa, Australasia, Europe, and North and South America. He is an existential-analytic psychotherapist, photographer, and chartered psychologist, and one of the first recipients of the Royal Photographic Society/GRIFO 'Diamond Phototherapy Award'. His books include *Phototherapy and Therapeutic Photography in a Digital Age* (2013 Routledge), and *Existential Psychotherapy and Counselling after Post-Modernism* (2017, Routledge). He is also Founding Editor of the *European Journal of Psychotherapy and Counselling* (Routledge) and has a private practice in England (Wimbledon and Brighton). www.delloewenthal.com

Acknowledgements

I am very fortunate to have so many people to thank!

Phototherapy and therapeutic photography have enabled me to bring together two of my life interests, namely, photography and psychotherapy. To start with photography: I first would like to acknowledge my family of birth's next door neighbour Mr Parr, a keen amateur photographer who, when I was a child, introduced me to the magic of black and white developing and printing. He not only led me to purchase a Voightlander Vito B camera and use his Rolleiflex but also taught me the discipline of practising each day to hold my camera and take dummy shots – film was so expensive! (I didn't have a light meter but could sometimes make good enough guesses, for example f8 at 1/125th!). The Voightlander was only supplanted when I was much older, in my mid-thirties, and my mother's brother Cecil Braine paid for my Nikon FM2, of which I still have the fondest memories with its 50 mm lens that came closest to the eye and my interests in phenomenology (and my denial of the 'constructed image'!).

I kept an interest in photography through most of my life with the help of evening courses at what I used to call Brighton Art College (thank you Zule!), unexpectedly doing a part-time BA degree in Photography and Multi-Media at the University of Westminster (with thanks especially to Tom Ang and Gus Wiley), formerly the Polytechnic of Central London (PCL). More recently, my thanks also go to staff (Lewis Bush, Peter Fraser, Max Houghton, and Paul Lowe) and students, this time from the University of the Arts /London College of communication MA in Documentary Photography and Photojournalism.

I would also like to add here many thanks regarding my project 'My father the Kristallnacht Carrier', which appears in various chapters, to my fellow student Rainer Eidemuller, and particularly to his mum for translating over 50 letters I found in the attic from old German to modern German and then into English. Further thanks to Gauri Chauhan for her assistance with all things digital (and without whose help this book would not have been possible); to Simon Sandys for helping me to relearn studio work (including developing & printing, Photoshop, and Lightroom); and to Liz Nicholl for help in transcribing. However, my greatest collaborators for that project are Eduard, Adele, and Hilde, for together with Grandma Loewe, I got to know them all through re-enactment phototherapy.

With regard to psychotherapy, I perhaps ought to start with founding relation-ships. So, my thanks go to my mother and particularly to my father for ensuring, besides a loving environment, that I mainly had to listen. Both my parents were compulsive talkers, wanting to talk without interruption (my father always took his breathes in the middle of sentences whereas my mother could start talking before she entered the room!).

I am also thankful to have been on the staff of one of the, if not the, first trainings in counselling in London at South West London College when I was still a student. Here, my particular thanks go to Gaie Houston and Bridget Proctor. I was later to train, and I think it took me over all at least 15 years to pass as an analytic psycho-therapist at the Philadelphia Association with particular thanks to Chris Oakley, Steve Gans, and John Heaton. I also must thank my fellow students of all the above, as so very much was learnt by being with them.

I want also to thank staff and students of the organisations where I established training and research organisations, namely, the Health and Social Management Unit (HASMU) at South West London College, the Managerial and Therapeutic Educational Research (MATER) Project and Centre for Therapeutic Education both at the University of Surrey; the Research Centre for Therapeutic Education (RCTE) at the University of Roehampton; and the Southern Association for Psy-chotherapy and Counselling (SAFPAC) where I'm currently Chair. Here, as else-where, there are so many more people to mention, including Erik Abrams, Betty Betrand, Diane Bray, Tom Davey, James Davies, Anastasios Gaitanidis, Jo Gee, Anne Guy, Dennis Greenwood, Helen McEwan, Jayne Redmond, Robert Snell, and Di Thomas. With special thanks to Julia Cayne and Onel Brooks, my long-standing colleagues, that includes, at this time of writing, our work together on SAFPAC's critical existential-analytic psychotherapy training.

This brings me to acknowledge those who particularly helped me with pho-totherapy and therapeutic photography. I must immediately thank Carmine Parella from Italy and Ulla Halkola and Tarja Koffert from Finland (and also from Finland, Leena Koulu, Mari Krappala, and Pirkko Pehunen) for teaching me so much when working on the EU Project PhototherapyEurope: Learning and Healing through Phototherapy (Leonardo da Vinci). Further thanks to Jonathan Isserow at the University of Roehampton, London, for his encouragement over many years to teach phototherapy and therapeutic photography for the MA in Art Psychotherapy.

Thank you also to my colleagues from Italy, Greece, Malta, Sweden, and the UK, including Evrinomy Avdi, Gauri Chauhan, Emanuela Saita, Tommi Natri, Roberto Righi, Adrian Tompea, Joseph Giordmaina, and Philia Issari when I was the Prin-cipal Researcher for the EU Project PhototherapyEurope in Prisons (Grundtvig).

Also, my thanks go out to the North American innovators Judy Weiser, Da-vid Krauss, and Joel Walker, whom I met in Finland and whose workshops I at-tended there. My further thanks extend to my co-contributors on the book I edited, *Phototherapy and Therapeutic Photography in a Digital Age* – Keith Kennedy, Terry Dennett, Mark Wheeler, Mike Simmons, Rosy Martin, Cristina Nunez, Carmine Parella, Rodolfo de Bernart, Julia Winckler, Alexander Kopytin, Hasse Karlsson, and Brigitte Anor – with all of whom I have also had, and in many cases still have, enhancing conversations.

Also, I extend my thanks for the work and resulting conversations I have been involved in with Neil Gibson, Ayres Marques Pinto, and Claire Craig.

I want particularly to thank the real pioneers of phototherapy and therapeutic photography – Hugh Diamond (I am the delighted recipient of a Hugh Diamond Phototherapy Award); Linda Berman, with whom I have had some correspondence; and Jo Spence. Regarding Jo Spence, I unfortunately never met her but have unknowingly followed some of her learning experiences at the Henderson Hospital, Polytechnic of Central London (PCL)/University of Westminster and John Heron's co-counselling training at Quaesitor and University of Surrey. However, I have been fortunate to have had conversations with the late Terry Dennett and in particular with Jo's co-collaborator and, importantly, innovator in her own right, Rosy Martin, who has helped me so much.

And last, but far from least, my special thanks go to my wife Jane for her love and support. So, I wish to thank everyone (particularly those I haven't named and very much including my clients) for what I have learnt from our times together whilst also stating that I take responsibility for this book.

Introduction

Photography as therapy

This handbook for therapists, photographers, other professionals, clients, and activist clients, amongst others includes, mainly with the use of case studies, the following major approaches to phototherapy and therapeutic photography:

- Talking Pictures Therapy
- Re-enactment phototherapy
- The taking of therapeutic photographs
- The creation of therapeutic Photobooks and photo stories
- Therapeutic photo diaries
- The use of Photocards in training, team, and management development
- The development of action plans through photography
- The therapeutic use of portraiture (including 'selfies')
- The use of photographs to explore ethical photographic and other practices
- Phototherapy and therapeutic photography theory
- Phototherapy and therapeutic photography research
- Facilitating emotional learning through phototherapy workshops

As a visual medium, photography would seem like a natural contender for therapeutic use, and yet its potential has been sparingly explored until now. In recent years, there has been renewed interest in phototherapy techniques – especially for clients who are strongly resistant to therapy and those who find it easier to communicate through visual aids. The field is especially relevant today, in an era of smartphones where a visual narrative of the client's feelings, memories, reactions, and thoughts exists as a series of photographs – potentially available to share with the therapist as a catalyst for therapeutic communication.

Rationale

There is a need for a book which:

- Locates all major approaches to phototherapy and therapeutic photography in one text
- Aids in learning by starting with exercises, key points, and actual case studies
- Is written for professionals, clients, and the self-help activist client

DOI: 10.4324/9781003240914-1

This publication particularly addresses the need of the psychological therapist meta-phorically to come alongside and work with clients in a digital era where, for example, digital photography, has become such a prevalent part of our culture. This will enable them to keep abreast of changes in our cultural practices to date such that clients can see what is being offered as relevant. However, there is not an existing publication which includes all major approaches to phototherapy and therapeutic photography in one text. This publication is also very much a self-help book for those people who wish to do self-exploration, either as an adjunct to their therapy or to carry out their own self-development. The book is designed with the aim that all of these readers can quickly inform themselves about particular approaches of current interest.

Despite the growing interest in phototherapy and therapeutic photography, there is a paucity of actual case studies. Such case studies are needed by both therapists and clients, but are not currently comprehensively available. The main reasons for the relative lack of case studies are probably ethical issues, in that even with agreement of the client, it is often considered unethical to publicly share the work, more so when the therapist feels obliged to be available for future therapeutic work with the client. However, this book provides such detailed case studies as a necessary aid to learning often through the author providing personal examples.

Who is the book for?

The readership for which this book is intended includes all psychological therapists and, in particular, psychotherapists, psychoanalysts, counsellors, psychologists, and arts therapists, as well as photographers, researchers, trainers, and others wishing to explore further the use of photographs therapeutically within their existing practices. Importantly, this book additionally addresses self-help for the client and activist client as an aid to self-development through carrying out phototherapy and therapeutic photography on themselves.

Style

Each chapter has a consistency in providing a summary, exercise, and key learning points, and is often case-study based. However, as the content varies from techniques/methods to research to theory, the writing styles vary accordingly. As many readers may be interested in any particular moment in certain aspects, this book is also written so the reader who wants to can dip into just those topics.

Why phototherapy and therapeutic photography?

In my previous book on this subject, I start with the quote, 'What is photography for? Can it change our minds?' (Dalley, 2008). This time I am responding with a more affirmative answer by first taking the ideas of Alain de Botton and John Armstrong (2013) from their book *Art as Therapy* and applying them to *Photography as Therapy*.

Alain de Botton and John Armstrong (2013: 57–58) argue that, as humans:

1. We forget what matters; we can't hold on to important but slippery experiences.
2. We have a proclivity to lose hope . . .
3. We incline towards feelings of isolation and persecution because we have an unrealistic sense of how much difficulty is normal. We panic . . . We are lonely . . . We suffer . . .
4. We are unbalanced and lose sight of our best sides . . .
5. We are hard to get to know: We are mysterious to ourselves and therefore no good at explaining who we are to others, or being liked for reasons we think are appropriate.
6. We reject many experiences, peoples, places and eras that have something important to offer us because they come in the wrong wrapping . . .
7. We are desensitised by familiarity and live in a commercially dominated world that highlights glamour . . .

de Botton and Armstrong (2013: 58–59) then suggest that, in response to what they regard as the aforementioned 'psychological frailties' that 'art finds its purpose and value as a tool, and offers us seven means of assistance'. I will now quote their 'seven means of assistance,' but replacing 'art' with 'photography':

1. *A corrective of bad memory*: [Photography] makes memorable and renewable the fruits of experience.
2. *A purveyor of hope*: [Photography] keeps pleasant and cheering things in view. It knows we despair too easily.
3. *A source of dignified sorrow*: [Photography] reminds us of the legitimate place of sorrow in a good life, so that we panic less about our difficulties and recognise them as parts of a noble existence.
4. A balancing agent: [Photography] encodes with unusual clarity the essence of our good qualities and holds them up before us, in a variety of media, to help rebalance our natures and direct us towards our best possibilities.
5. *A guide to self-knowledge*: [Photography] can help us identify what is central to ourselves, but hard to put into words. Much that is human is not readily available in language. We can hold up [a photograph] and say, confusedly but importantly, 'This is me'.
6. A guide to the extension of experience: [Photographs can be] an immensely sophisticated accumulation of the experiences of others, presented to us in well-shaped and well-organised forms. It can provide us with some of the most eloquent instances of the voices of other cultures, so that an engagement with [photography] stretches our notions of ourselves and our world.
7. *A re-sensitisation tool*: [Photography] peels away our shell and saves us from our spoilt, habitual disregard for what is all around us. We recover our sensitivity; we look at the old in new ways. We are prevented from assuming that novelty and glamour are the only solutions.

These points are proposed as some of the reasons why more people are turning to phototherapy and therapeutic photography (we will later be looking at scientific explorations of their efficacy). This handbook is designed to take the reader through different ways in which phototherapy and therapeutic photography can provide such a 'means of assistance' for our 'psychological frailties' by facilitating the personal development of ourselves and others.

References

Dalley, J. (2008). The first prix pictet. *Financial Times*, 1 November.
de Botton, A., and Armstrong, J. (2013). *Art as Therapy*. London: Phaidon.

1 An overview of phototherapy and therapeutic photography

For the psychological therapist and other professionals, activist clients, and clients

Summary

This chapter introduces phototherapy and therapeutic photography and distinguishes between various approaches to the therapeutic use of photographs. Furthermore, described in this chapter is the way in which the handbook can be used by psychological therapists (counsellors, psychotherapists, psychoanalysts, psychologists, arts and play therapists, and other professionals), as well as clients, including activist self-help clients. Each of the main approaches to phototherapy and therapeutic photography, which are covered in the subsequent chapters, are then introduced.

Key learning points

1. There can be seen to be five main methods regarding the therapeutic use of photographs:

   - The therapeutic use of Photocards (most often called 'phototherapy')
   - The taking of therapeutic photographs (most often called 'therapeutic photography'), which can include photo diaries and re-enactment phototherapy
   - The therapeutic creation of Photobooks
   - The development of action plans through photography
   - The therapeutic use of portraiture (including 'selfies')

2. Photocards can also be used to aid elicitation in such professions as management and team development and more generally enable discussion of difficult topics.
3. Regarding research: Phototherapy and therapeutic photography can both be seen as conducting research in their own right and benefit from research methods in the psychological therapies.
4. Photographs can be used to help phototherapists and professionals develop their practices ethically.
5. The practicing phototherapist needs to be a trained psychological therapist having had their own therapy.
6. Therapeutic photography is best practised by the self-help activist client or trained psychological therapist, unless the facilitation is only technical.

DOI: 10.4324/9781003240914-2

7. In training phototherapists and therapeutic photographers (and in facilitating emotional learning through phototherapy and therapeutic photography workshops), whilst the theory behind their effectiveness can be seen as psychoanalytical, person-centred therapy (with its emphasis on reflecting what is said and underlying feelings) is recommended.

Exercise

Choose any photograph that calls to you. It can be one you've taken or one you've found. Now, write a couple of sentences explaining why you chose that photo.

Distinguishing phototherapy from therapeutic photography

Phototherapy can be broadly defined as the use of photographs within psychotherapy, where therapists will use techniques to enable clients to express their concerns during counselling sessions (Krauss and Fryrear 1983). Whereas **therapeutic photography** often involves self-initiated, photo-based activities conducted by a person, and sometimes without a therapist guiding the experience, for self-exploration and personal growth (Martin and Spence 1987, 1988; Spence 1986).

This can be seen as taking photographs to work through what might be considered an emotional constriction. In practice, the distinctions between phototherapy and therapeutic photography are not always clear, and some practitioners use the methods interchangeably within their practice.

However, one of the main differences between phototherapy and therapeutic photography is that the former requires a trained therapist who has had their own one-to-one interpersonal therapy. This helps minimise the danger of the phototherapist unconsciously providing their own associations and projecting their unexplored emotional minefields onto the client. However, as mentioned, there sometimes appears to be at best a fine line between phototherapy and therapeutic photography. It would therefore appear vital that facilitators are aware of not inadvertently providing therapy requiring therapeutic training and wrongly calling it 'therapeutic photography'. Indeed, it is considered vital to be aware that 'therapeutic photography' is only ethically appropriate when either the practitioner and client are one and the same, as with the self-help activist client, or the facilitator stays completely away from any reflections or interpretations of the photographs.

Context and brief history

Phototherapy (which in the context of this book does not mean 'light therapy') and therapeutic photography are not separate entities but may be classed as existing on the continuum of photo-based healing practices. In turn, the two practices involve making use of the 'emotional-communication qualities of photographs and people's interactions with them' (Weiser 2004: 1). This is to enable clients to begin to speak of difficulties they experience that are otherwise difficult to talk about (Weiser 1993 [1999], 2001). These approaches can be seen as a form of photo-elicitation (Lapenta

2011), with its quality (Harper 2002) of enabling images creating 'possibilities for different observers to interpret according to their views' (Collier and Collier 1986: 103–108). The focus in this chapter and book is on the therapeutic use of photographs as methods for both the helping and related professions to enable their clients, and self-help activist clients to elicit words for themselves.

Following the groundbreaking work of Hugh Diamond (1856) and later European pioneers (Spence 1986; Berman 1993), much of the subsequent development of phototherapy initially took place in North America (for example Weiser 1993 [1999]; Krauss 2009). Since then, there have been developments in Europe, including the United Kingdom. This has brought further innovations, particularly in Finland and in such countries as Germany, Israel, Italy, Lithuania, Russia, Spain, and The Netherlands. This history was brought together for the first time in my book, *Phototherapy and Therapeutic Photography in a Digital Age* Loewenthal (2013b). However, that book was not, unlike this one, designed as a handbook.

Regarding the therapeutic approach: Within therapy, photographs can be seen *psychoanalytically* as a route to the unconscious, with the meanings clients attach to the photograph assumed to be the result of the client's projections and what may have been previously repressed. Repression is taken to be an unconscious exclusion of memories, impulses, desires and thoughts that are too difficult or unacceptable to deal with in consciousness – 'the essence of repression lies simply in turning something away and keeping it at a distance from the conscious' (Freud 1915: 147). In turn, for Freud (1914: 16), 'the theory of repression is the corner-stone on which the whole structure of psychoanalysis rests'. Consequently, photographs may be seen as devices through which the client's repressed projections can be realised within the therapy. The phototherapist does not need to work psychoanalytically; however, for those particularly interested, see Linda Berman's book, *Beyond the Smile* (1993).

In practice, a more humanistic modality appears most prevalent for those involved with this work, even though initial primacy is given to projective techniques. In fact, a *humanistic approach* based on the work of Carl Rogers (Rogers 1961; Mearns and Thorne 2013) is recommended, especially for those relatively new to therapeutic practice. Here, the phototherapist in particular:

• Reflects on what the client is saying without leaving anything out that is particularly important for the client and not adding in anything the client has not said
• Reflects back *occasionally* on what the phototherapist considers the client is feeling
• Shares *very occasionally* what the client is saying makes the phototherapist feel

All three types of interventions are offered very tentatively and attempt to enable clients to go in their own direction and not the one the phototherapist thinks is best.

What I have termed **'Talking Pictures Therapy'** (see Photo 1.1) may be spoken of as the use of photographs within the various counselling and psychotherapy modalities – *a process where the use of photographs may be incorporated into any psychological therapy that aims to enable clients to speak of what is of concern to them*, for example, person-centred, existential, and psychodynamic approaches (Loewenthal 2013b).

Photo 1.1 Talking Picture Cards

As described in my previous phototherapy book (Loewenthal 2013b: 5), the cultural importance of photographs has been well located elsewhere (for example, Barthes 1980; Sontag 1990). Freud also used photographs in order to caution his overenthusiastic disciples and to remind them of their task. It is said that he had two photographs on his desk: one of a patient looking 'well, hopeful, and healthy' at the commencement of therapy, and the other of a patient at the end of therapy looking 'dejected, depressed, and beaten by life' (Symington 1986: 25). Freud also encouraged his patients to bring him their dreams. So, as Brigitte Anor (see also, Anor 2013 in Loewenthal 2013b) once remarked to me, 'wouldn't it be helpful for them also to bring us their photographs?'

Importantly, we are now in the digital era, where the growth of digital photography, together with the rapid use of photography on social networking sites, ensures that phototherapy and therapeutic photography now represent major therapeutic opportunities.

Five main methods

As introduced in Loewenthal (2020), from others and my own practices (Loewenthal 2013a, 2013b, 2015a, 2015b; Loewenthal et al. 2015), five main methods for using photographs to help clients find their voice are delineated, and can overlap:

- The therapeutic use of photographs/Photocards (most often called 'phototherapy')
- The taking of therapeutic photographs (most often called 'therapeutic photography')
- The therapeutic creation of Photobooks
- The development of action plans through photography
- The therapeutic use of portraiture (including 'selfies')

All of these therapeutic photographic methods can be seen as researching participants' emotional learning (Quigley and Barrett 1999) to help evolve, clarify, and communicate feelings and thoughts. Furthermore, these approaches can be used on a one-to-one basis or in a group. They will be explored in the following chapters but first, as a bridge, they will now be described further:

1. The use of Photocards (most often called 'phototherapy')

This is the subject of *Chapter 2: Phototherapy and Talking Pictures Therapy*. The chapter focuses on three main areas in showing how photographs can be used in current counselling/psychotherapy practices. Initially, brief case study vignettes are provided showing how clients can respond to choosing the initial photograph from a set. Then, the specific use of Photocards in therapy is provided through case studies of clients in a school. Thirdly, the use of client-found photographs, such as in reminiscence therapy, is considered.

To give some more detail of the case studies in this chapter and the research behind them: The initial focus here is on the therapeutic use of photographs within counselling and psychotherapy. The first case study given is a young offender's male prison (where the age range varies from 18 years to early 20s) in the south of England which provides a counselling service as part of its mental health services (and not as part of education, as in some other countries). Four young men who were

interested in having up to six sessions of counselling were informed that the therapeutic use of photographs was an option. The counselling provided in these cases
might be described as 'post-existential' (Loewenthal 2011), though this 'Talking
Pictures Therapy' can be used with any talking therapy where it is possible to ask
the client to choose a photograph that calls to them from a set and then to describe
what it was that made them select the particular image. The research I led on evaluating this young offender's male prison Loewenthal et al. (2015) included the use of
thematic analysis (Braun and Clarke 2006) and showed that over 90% of participants
found the use of Photocards 'very helpful' or 'helpful'.

Next, I focus on a school setting (Loewenthal 2013a) to evaluate Talking Pictures Therapy (the therapeutic use of photographs within counselling and psychotherapy). For those readers interested in research (see Chapter 12), qualitative
and quantitative methods, including the use of children's choice of photographs
in terms of visual research, were used. With regard to qualitative research, a collective case study method was again utilised as the research approach based on
Greenwood and Loewenthal (2005, 2007), where Husserlian bracketing is combined with hermeneutics; the study was strongly influenced by Bleicher's (1980)
work on the phenomenology of Heidegger and Gadamer. We, in turn, developed
this further from Yin's (1984) consideration of case study method as a means of
generalisation.

Patient health questionnaire-9 (PHQ-9) (for depression), generalised anxiety
disorder-7 (GAD-7) (for anxiety), and the improving access to psychological
therapies (IAPT) phobia scale (IAPT minimum data set), together with the overall measure clinical outcomes in routine evaluation-10 (CORE-10) were used for
quantitative assessment.

These case studies indicated how quickly Photocards can enable clients to say
what is on their minds. As Martin describes, '. . . photographs provide an unfiltered
connection with the unconscious since what takes place within the phototherapy
session is rooted in unconscious processes' (Martin 2013, in Loewenthal 2013b).

2. The taking of therapeutic photographs (most often called 'therapeutic photography')

This method, which can particularly lend itself to the self-help activist client, is
considered in several chapters. First, in *Chapter 3: Therapeutic photography*, the focus
is on two case studies of therapeutic photography. What is primarily provided are
the photographs for both these case studies and a description of the process undertaken. 'Putting the (m)other first' demonstrates how therapeutic photography can
be utilised to work through loss and grief. In this case, the photographs are of the
author's childhood home upon the death of his mother. Here, a further question is
examined on whether the photographer is putting himself or his mother first when
photographically working through his grief. The second case involves the author
coming to terms with, and working through, depression and exhaustion.

Then in *Chapter 5: Re-enactment phototherapy*, I explore re-enactment phototherapy through describing how my father never recovered from the loss of his parents

and sister in the Holocaust to the extent that he could not talk about his family, nor want anything of value, which partly included his family (and me!). Utilising re-enactment phototherapy, I dressed as my father, grandfather, grandmother, and aunt based on a photograph of each that my father originally brought to England together with an extraordinary amount of his mother's Czech crystal. Through this photographic exploration, I started to tell in their voice their story as I imagined it from when my father left Czechoslovakia to the moment of his, and what were to become my, family's deaths. Already things were changing, I had never previously called them 'my grandfather, grandmother, and aunt', but rather 'my father's parents and sister'. Now, with trepidation, and through this re-enactment phototherapy, they were becoming 'Eduard', 'Adele' and Hilde'.

This is an example following the work of Jo Spence (Dennett (2013) and Martin (2013) (both in Loewenthal 2013b). The research of this form of therapeutic photography, which also was influenced by Moustakas's (1990) heuristic research and Hirsch's (2012) post-memory, enabled the author to bring them alive so he could more appropriately psychologically bury them.

I have put this re-enactment phototherapy under 'therapeutic photography'; however, it would need to go under 'phototherapy' if there is facilitation of the client that involved any kind of intervention other than technical. Given it is extremely difficult to not consciously, and particularly unconsciously, convey anything to a client, it is strongly recommended that re-enactment or any therapeutic photography is best carried out by the self-help activist client on themselves. It can then be called therapeutic photography; otherwise, it should be named 'phototherapy' and facilitated by a trained therapist.

The same is true for the subject of *Chapter 6: Therapeutic photo diaries*. Here, a case is given showing the use of a photo diary regarding the author's exploration of the personal, the political, and the professional as a result of the COVID lockdown. As the chapter starts:

> At the start of COVID, my wife and I were separated through working at different locations when the travel curfew came into force. This was for by far the longest time (over 14 weeks) in over 40 years for us not to be together. During this enforced separation, I kept a photo diary through taking a daily photograph with my phone. The first photo I took (when doing my then newly initiated habit of jogging) was of two shorn off trees. As with the metaphor of what had happened with the trees, so much had been and was to be shorn off our lives through COVID.

3. The therapeutic creation of Photobooks

The context for the approach described here (Loewenthal 2015a) is the use of Photobooks in a medium-to-high security male prison in the South of England. Here, working as a group or individually, inmates who were fathers were asked to choose photos from the 52 Talking Pictures Photocards in response to questions devised and posed by the author in order to individually make books for their children. What is also important in the making of the book is what is therapeutically said in the making process. For example, one inmate, whom I have called Fernandez (Loewenthal 2015a), was known as having a particularly high suicide risk, but while therapeutically working on the Photobook for his son, it preventatively emerged that he was suicidal because when he previously was a mercenary, he had killed boys his son's age.

Hence, *Chapter 4: The creation of therapeutic Photobooks* provides case studies of working with individuals and groups to create Photobooks as a means of emotional development. Two forms of Photobooks are considered. The first, Talking Picture Books, explored in depth, is where the client writes a personal book for an actual or imagined person, choosing photographs followed by brief descriptions to assist what they want to say. The second type of book, story books, is one where a story is created using photographs for an important other to read. The case studies chosen are taken from prison inmates writing these books for their children.

4. The therapeutic use of portraiture (including 'selfies')

The taking of selfies appears to be an increasingly significant cultural practice. Through phototherapy, there are increasing possibilities for their use. For example, I have used them therapeutically to enable clients to explore 'what I like and don't like about myself' (why the reject button is used). Christina Nunez (2013), in Loewenthal (2013b), importantly writes about self-portraits, including photo diaries, as a means of personal development.

5. The development of action plans through photography

A well-established use of photography in this way is provided by PhotoVoice, one of whose projects they commissioned the author to evaluate (Loewenthal and Clark 2013). Interestingly, PhotoVoice was considered excellent in their facilitators not working as therapists and therefore this could then also be seen as under the banner of therapeutic photography. However, some of the inmates said they missed someone to explore what the photos they took meant, in which case a trained therapist would be required, as in phototherapy (see Chapter 2). PhotoVoice trains individuals and interest groups to use photography to bring about social change. A development stemming from this was devised by the author whereby participants either take photographs or use Photocards to develop action plans which can vary, for example, from gaining employment (Loewenthal 2015a) to coming out as gay. Here, participants are facilitated to combine photography with a form of force field analysis (Lewin 1943).

Thus, in *Chapter 8: The development of action plans through photography*, a case is given of the author working with a group of ex-inmates who have been given a forensic diagnosis and have joined this photographic group in order to find employment. Over two weekends, the group were briefly introduced to taking photographs with point and shoot cameras. This was followed by an exploration of external forces to them, and then their internal forces, that they perceived as helping and hindering getting a job. As part of this process, participants took photographs in order to help them clarify these internal and external forces. Then, through the use of force field analysis, they were able to prioritise which actions would be most productive in helping them get a job and which forces diminished their chances of getting work. A case study of one of the participants is provided.

The five therapeutic photographic methods mentioned earlier, which can be carried out on a one-to-one basis or in a group, can be seen as helping participants evolve, clarify, and communicate their feelings and thoughts, hence promoting their emotional learning (Quigley and Barrett 1999).

Photocard elicitation: Discussion groups, training, and management and team development

This handbook has further chapters. For one, Photocards can be used for elicitation in development contexts that are not directly therapeutic. Thus, there are forms of elicitation that, whilst similar, should not be regarded as either phototherapy or therapeutic photography. Hence, *Chapter 7* explores *Professional and personal development: The use of photography in coaching, training, and team and management development*. In this chapter, the primary focus is on the author's work with an international company that commissions expensive processing plants throughout the world. The problem which the Photocards were designed to solve involved project managers who were normally engineers needing to have more of the language of the various stakeholders to further ensure that the upfront design met the stakeholders' needs. Otherwise, there was a very real danger that if the plant was mainly designed from an engineering perspective, that subsequent changes once commissioning had started, could easily lead to a highly significant increase in the reconstruction costs. Photocards were used in one-to-one meetings with project managers to enable them to develop their abilities to communicate with stakeholders from the initiation of the planning process. Further consideration is given to the use of Photocards to enable groups to explore difficult topics through training and team development.

Ethics, theory, research, and training in phototherapy and therapeutic photography

The chapters referred to earlier are primarily practice-based. Three other areas, each designated a specific chapter, are further explored in this handbook. They include ethics; theory, research and evaluation; and training in phototherapy and therapeutic photography. Hence, the title of *Chapter 10* is *Can phototherapy and therapeutic photography be practices of ethics?*

Here such questions are explored as: What helps or hinders an exploration of the most effective expressions of phototherapists' and therapeutic photographers' (as well as psychotherapists' and photographers') desire to help? Is it possible to have both justice and action? In examining issues of phototherapy and therapeutic photography as practices of ethics in terms of ideas of truth, justice, and responsibility, is there a contemporary ethical basis on which we can assist in an embodied way so that we can help others not do violence to others? Indeed, is it possible for us as phototherapists and therapeutic photographers, (psychotherapists, photographers, etc.) not to interrupt our own and others' continuity, not to play roles in which we no longer recognise ourselves and whereby we betray not only our commitments but our own substance? In particular, what is explored is: What does it mean then for the person who is the psychotherapist, photographer, etc. to put the person who is the client (or photographed) first?

Also importantly, the photographer's ethical framework, illustrated with the ethics of famous photographers, provided in this chapter has been found to be helpful in enabling students and professionals of other practices such as education, psychological therapies, and management (Freud's three impossible professions) to consider their own ethics.

Chapter 11 gives overview of approaches to *Phototherapy and therapeutic photography: Theory, research, and evaluation.* A case study is then provided of the use of theory and research in evaluating the therapeutic effectiveness of Talking Pictures Therapy in the context, as referred to in Chapter 2, of working in schools. The focus is on photographs used in brief psychotherapy and counselling with the purpose of enabling clients to express and explore aspects of their lives they would like to talk about. The author presents examples using Talking Pictures Therapy in brief therapy with children aged 12 to 14 years old in a UK school setting. The use of photographs is discussed further as an evaluative measure in assessing the client's 'progress' through their choice and resulting descriptions of the photographs chosen, as compared with standardised measures of client progress.

Throughout, as with psychotherapy and counselling, there is the argument that photo therapy and therapeutic photography are the research! Thus, whilst the first examples of my research mentioned earlier particularly focus on the effectiveness of phototherapy as a method, within this, through participants' choice of photograph and the meanings they attach to them, it may be as important to consider phototherapy as a different method of research. Thus, the potential of the use of photographs as an evaluation of therapeutic change seems particularly worthy of further development and use given that, as mentioned, photography has become so much more a part of everyday life with the advent of smart phones and social media. Hence, using photographs as a potential evaluation of therapeutic change may be a beneficial and complementary if not an alternative approach to evaluation approaches such as GAD-7, PHQ-9, and CORE-10.

So, in this chapter, there is the argument that it would appear not only that the therapeutic digital use of photographs may need to consider other psychotherapeutic research being conducted more generally in the psychological therapies but also that photography can provide a new form of therapeutic practice and research.

This book concludes with *Chapter 12: Bringing it all together: Training yourself and others as phototherapists and therapeutic photographers and facilitating workshops.*

The focus here is the training of phototherapy and therapeutic photography practitioners. Examples are provided of both how this can be integrated into existing programmes for training counsellors, psychotherapists, psychologists, arts and play therapists and how a five-day programme was provided for related professions working in European criminal justice systems.

The case study given describes a phototherapy and therapeutic photography workshop with a group of young LGBT+ participants who had come together as one of the participants said, with general agreement *'to understand myself and people around me'.*

The training of the five main approaches outlined earlier are described (they might more often be singularly used within a traditional one-on-one therapy session rather than as here employed together over five weekly sessions with a group).

The chapter concludes by exploring issues in the training of phototherapy and therapeutic photography practitioners followed by some thoughts on current and future phototherapy and therapeutic photography practices.

Conclusion

These approaches of phototherapy and therapeutic photography that allow what the photograph chosen by the disembodied client brings to this client's mind have the advantage of phenomenologically or post-phenomenologically (Cayne and Loewenthal 2011) allowing something to emerge which is not pre-defined by, for example, a medicalised model of diagnosis and treatment, and hence not starting with a pre-determined notion of, for example, clinical success.

This change in language through digital photography changes culturally what, and how, we experience, not only in terms of being able to look back on such websites as Facebook as to what photos we and others posted of ourselves, but to the very nature of our experiences. Perhaps this change in our way of perceiving and thinking will be even greater than when photography, at the start of the 20th century, changed the perception and thinking of so many people, including Sigmund Freud (Bergstein 2010).

In conclusion, this handbook has been designed as outlined in this chapter to provide a guide for the self-help activist, psychological therapist, and various professionals to develop their therapeutic practices using photography.

References

Anor, B. (2013). Epilogue. Hands up – surrender to subjectivity. In D. Loewenthal (ed.), *Phototherapy and Therapeutic Photography in a Digital Age*, pp. 177–179. Hove: Routledge.

Barthes, R. (1980). *Camera Lucida: Reflections on Photography*. New York: Hill & Wang.

Bergstein, M. (2010). *Mirrors of Memory: Freud, Photography and the History of Art*. London: Cornell University Press.

Berman, L. (1993). *Beyond the Smile*. London: Routledge.

Bleicher, J. (1980). *Contemporary Hermeneutics*. London: Routledge & Kegan Paul.

Braun, V., and Clarke, V. (2006). Using thematic analysis in psychology. *Qualitative Research in Psychology*, 3: 77–101.

Cayne, J., and Loewenthal, D. (2011). Post-phenomenology and the between as unknown. In D. Loewenthal (ed.), *Post-Existentialism and the Psychological Therapies: Towards a Therapy Without Foundations*. Abingdon: Routledge.

Collier, J., and Collier, M. (1986). *Visual Anthropology: Photography as a Research Method*. Albuquerque: University of New Mexico Press.

Dennett, T. (2013). Chapter 3, Jo Spence's camera therapy: Personal therapeutic photography as a response to adversity. In D. Loewenthal (ed.), *Phototherapy and Therapeutic Photography in a Digital Age*, pp. 31–39. Hove: Routledge.

Diamond, H. (1856). On the application of photography to the physiognomic and mental phenomena of insanity. *Proceedings of the Royal Society of London*, 8: 117. Reprinted in Gilman, S. (ed.). (2014). *Face of Madness: Hugh W. Diamond and the Origin of Psychiatric Photography*, pp. 17–24. Brattleboro, VT: Echo Point Books & Media.

Freud, S. (1914). On the history of the psycho-analytic movement. *Standard Edition*, 14: 7–66.

Freud, S. (1915). Repression. *Standard Edition*, 14: 141–158.

Greenwood, D., and Loewenthal, D. (2005). Case study as a means of researching social work and improving practitioner education. *Journal of Social Work Practice*, 19(2): 181–193.

Greenwood, D., and Loewenthal, D. (2007). A case of case study method: The possibility of psychotherapy with a person diagnosed with dementia. In D. Loewenthal (ed.), *Case Studies in Relational Research*, pp. 88–113. Basingstoke: Palgrave Macmillan.

Harper, D. (2002). Talking about pictures: A case for photo elicitation. *Visual Studies*, 17(1).

Hirsch, M. (2012). *The Generation of Postmemory: Writing and Visual Culture After the Holocaust*. New York: Columbia University Press.

Krauss, D. (2009). *Phototherapy and Reminiscence with the Elderly: Photo-Reminiscence*. Unpublished paper given at the 2009 International Symposium on PhotoTherapy and Therapeutic Photography, Turku, Finland, 11 June.

Krauss, D., and Fryrear, J. (1983). *Phototherapy in Mental Health*. Springfield, IL: Charles C. Thomas Pub Ltd.

Lapenta, F. (2011). Geomedia: On location-based media, the changing status of collective image production and the emergence of social navigation systems. *Visual Studies*, 26(1): 14–22.

Lewin, K. (1943). Defining the 'field at a given time'. *Psychological Review*, 50(3): 292–310. Republished (1997). *Resolving Social Conflicts & Field Theory in Social Science*. Washington, DC: American Psychological Association.

Loewenthal, D. (2011). *Post-Existentialism and the Psychological Therapies: Towards a Therapy without Foundations*. London: Karnac.

Loewenthal, D. (2013a). Talking pictures therapy as brief therapy in a school setting. *Journal of Creativity in Mental Health*, 8: 21–34.

Loewenthal, D. (ed.). (2013b). *Phototherapy and Therapeutic Photography in a Digital Age*. Hove: Routledge.

Loewenthal, D. (2015a). The therapeutic use of photographs in the United Kingdom criminal justice system. *European Journal of Counselling and Psychotherapy*, 17(1): 39–56.

Loewenthal, D. (2015b). Counselling and psychotherapy in the UK: The story of Winston. In R. Moodley, M. Sookoor, U. Gielen, and R. H. Wu (eds.), *Therapy Without Borders: International and Cross-Cultural Case Studies*. Alexandria, VA: American Counseling Association (ACA).

Loewenthal, D. (2020). The therapeutic use of photography: Phototherapy and therapeutic photography. In L. Pauwels and D. Mannay (eds.), *Sage Handbook of Visual Research Methods*, 2nd edition. London: Sage.

Loewenthal, D., and Clark, D. (2013). *Evaluation of PhotoVoice 'Shutter Release Project'*. London: University of Roehampton.

Loewenthal, D. et al. (2015). Evaluating the therapeutic use of photographs in European prisons. *Counselling Psychology Quarterly*, 30(1): 68–75.

Martin, R. (2013). Inhabiting the image: Photography, therapy and re-enactment photography. In D. Loewenthal (ed.), *Phototherapy and Therapeutic Photography in a Digital Age*, pp. 69–81. Hove: Routledge.

Martin, R., and Spence, J. (1987). *Double Exposure: The Minefield of Memory*. London: Photographer's Gallery (Exhibition and Catalogue).

Martin, R., and Spence, J. (1988). Phototherapy as a healing art. In L. Wells (ed.), *The Photography Reader*. London and New York: Routledge.

Mearns, D., and Thorne, B. (2013). *Person-Centred Counselling in Action*. London: Sage.

Moustakas, C. (1990). *Heuristic Research: Design, Methodology, and Applications*. London: Sage.

Nunez, C. (2013). The self-portrait as self-therapy In D. Loewenthal (ed.), *Phototherapy and Therapeutic Photography in a Digital Age*, pp. 95–106. Hove: Routledge.

Quigley, K., and Barrett, L. (1999). Emotional learning and mechanics of international psychological change. In J. Brandstaedter and R. Learner (eds.), *Action and Self Development: Theory and Research Through the Life Span*. Thousand Oaks, CA: Sage.

Rogers, C. (1961). *On Becoming a Person: A Therapist's View of Psychotherapy*. Boston: Houghton Mifflin.

Sontag, S. (1990). *On Photography*. New York: Anchor.

Spence, J. (1986). *Putting Myself in the Picture: A Political, Personal and Photographic Autobiography*. London: Camden Press.

Symington, N. (1986). *The Analytic Experience: Lectures from the Tavistock*. London: Free Association Books.

Weiser, J. (1993 [1999]). *Phototherapy Techniques: Exploring the Secrets of Personal Snapshots and Family Albums*, 2nd edition. Vancouver: Phototherapy Centre.

Weiser, J. (2001). PhotoTherapy techniques: Using clients' personal snapshots and family photos as counselling and therapy tools. *Afterimage: The Journal of Media Arts and Cultural Criticism*, 29(3): 10–15.

Weiser, J. (2004). Phototherapy techniques in counselling and therapy – using ordinary snapshots and photo-interactions to help clients heal their lives. *The Canadian Art Therapy Association Journal*, 17(2): 23–53.

Yin, R. (1984). *Case Study Research: Design and Methods*, 1st edition. Beverly Hills, CA: Sage.

2 Phototherapy and Talking Pictures Therapy

Summary

This chapter focuses on three main areas that show how photographs can be used in current counselling/psychotherapeutic practices. Initially, brief case study vignettes are provided showing how clients can respond to choosing an initial photograph from a set. Then, the specific use of Photocards in therapy is discussed through case studies of clients in a school. Thirdly, the use of client-found photographs, such as in reminiscence therapy, is examined.

Key learning points

1. Ensure that your client is aware before you start that Talking Pictures Therapy is available as part of the counselling/therapy you are offering.
2. In choosing or creating a set of Photocards, it is recommended not to use ones of people but rather of fairly simple objects and scenes. I have created the names 'Talking Pictures Therapy' and 'Talking Pictures', which I use here, but any set of about 50 photos can be used.
3. At the start of the session, getting the client to help put the Talking Pictures on the floor or a table can be a useful icebreaker.
4. It is recommended to keep your distance as the therapist by sitting opposite, rather than alongside, your client.
5. Ask the client, 'Which photo calls to you?' and then 'Why did you choose that card?'.
6. Be prepared in the session and subsequent sessions to use Talking Pictures variably, from asking the client to choose another photo to never referring, at least directly, to the Talking Pictures again.
7. What is important is to work with your client in whatever therapeutic modality you have been trained in and use the Photocards as an adjunct. There is not a separate profession entitled 'phototherapist', rather it is an additional speciality for the counsellor, psychoanalyst, psychotherapist, psychologist, psychiatrist, arts and play therapist, etc.
8. The choice of Talking Pictures with the client's description of their context can provide a method to evaluate the therapy, as can asking workshop group

DOI: 10.4324/9781003240914-3

participants to choose a Talking Picture that describes their experience of the event (see Chapter 12).

Exercise

Choose one photo from a set, for example, one of the 52 Talking Pictures (located at: www.delloewenthal.com/phototherapy-and-therapeutic-photography.html) that calls to you. Describe why you chose that photo.

Phototherapy

Phototherapy can broadly be defined as 'the use of photographs within psychotherapy, where therapists will use techniques to enable clients to express their concerns during counselling sessions' (Krauss and Fryrear 1983).

Judy Weiser (1999: 13–23) describes what she terms 'the five techniques of phototherapy':

1. The projective process
2. Working with self-portraits
3. Working with photos of clients taken by other people
4. Working with photos taken or collected by clients
5. Working with family albums and other autobiographical photos

The descriptions herein of Talking Pictures Therapy can be seen as corresponding to 'the projective process', whereas the other four methods can be seen as relying on client-found rather than therapist-found photos. For all five methods, what in my experience is most appropriate is for the therapist to explore the photos with the client in a 'person-centred' (Rogers 1995) way, as described in Chapter 1. Here, one tentatively reflects:

- What the client is saying
- What the client is feeling (occasionally)
- What the client is making one feel (even more occasionally)

This is easier to outline than to do! It can be seen as a phenomenological approach of the therapist (stemming from the work of Husserl, Heidegger, and Merleau-Ponty) which might be summarised (with thanks to Spinelli 2005) for the therapist to:

1. Encourage the client to keep describing rather than attempting to explain
2. Attempt to not have any preconceived, overarching idea of anything being more important than anything else
3. Bracket personal experiences and what you would do in the client's shoes

The theory here is that if therapists can work in this way, clients will become more aware and will then automatically, individually do what is best for themselves (as, in a different context, if one is aware of how one is sitting, then one changes to a more appropriate posture).

The initial Talking Picture photographs in phototherapy

Talking Pictures Therapy is an approach to brief therapy and counselling in which photographs are used to help clients express and explore aspects of their lives. The focus here is on the therapeutic use of photographs within counselling and psychotherapy. The first case of vignettes given herein are from a young offender's male prison (where the age range varies from eighteen years to early twenties) in England which provides counselling as part of their mental health services (and not as part of education, as in some other countries (Loewenthal et al. 2015)). This prison found four young men who were interested in having the up to six sessions of counselling and were informed that the therapeutic use of photographs was an option. The counselling provided might be described as 'post-existential' (Loewenthal 2011), though it can be used with any talking therapy where it is possible to ask the client to choose a photograph that calls to them and then describe what it was that made them do this.

The following examples includes the photographs that each of four young men chose from the 52 Talking Picture Cards (located at delloewenthal.com/photography) at the start of their therapy and what each then said. There are various other sets of Photocards available, and readers can also create them themselves from either found or their own photographs.

The names and identifying features of all those mentioned in this chapter (and throughout this book) have been changed, and all participants gave permission for the research and publication.

Jake

This 22-year-old man, with a small-medium build, looked much older than his age and was particularly difficult to hear. Jake said,

> . . . the only other possible photo is this one (Photo 2.1a). Love is a gift – you're still going to love someone because of who you are. Some people are born to be greedy – you can't change it. Love is more important – the stones are different colours, we all get close to each other – it's a heart shape. Get it? You get it? I've never loved anyone so much as my daughter . . . my mum brought me over from Africa when I was 14. I never knew who my father was. My mum said I couldn't go to school as she had lost my passport. Her bag was stolen. So, when I was 15, I left home, and I could only afford to stay with my friends who involved me in crime, and I would have been thrown out if I hadn't gone along with them. My partner is a good woman, but she is staying in a hostel. I don't know where we'll stay when I leave prison. I do need to fight back, otherwise I'm a victim allowing other people to put a knife in your back.

Photo 2.1a Jake's first photograph

Photo 2.1b Frank's first photograph

Photo 2.1c Mickey's first photograph

Photo 2.1d Dan's first photograph

[Jake then lifted his t-shirt showing eight stab wounds he received whilst living on the street.]

Frank

When I met this 22-year-old, he looked pale and withdrawn.

> I chose the photo of the beach (Photo 2.1b) because I've never been on holiday – I like nature. I went to see my dad in Wales when I was eight or nine, but after a couple of weeks, my dad said I couldn't stay and never meant to make for that to happen; they just made it up in order to try and make me behave better. When I was 13, I was going to see him again and I could have gone by train and somebody could have picked me up the other end, but my dad had diabetes and died. I tried to get my mum's approval, but then I was breaking the law and doing drugs. The youngest son of my mum has a different dad, as [do] the two in the middle. My mum moved from London to get me away, but it was a dead-end town with people doing drugs, and I started to do Class A and the offences were more serious. I met a girl when I was 14/15. She was a proper girlfriend, but eventually we split up and I couldn't deal with it. I self-harmed more, and so we moved to a council house in another area. I used to wake up every day and no-one was in the house other than my little brother and I got wound up and cut myself deep really bad. Went to hospital and hostel and then foster family. I thought I could not trust another girl again.

Mickey

Mickey was 20 years old and his appearance to me was of a crumpled figure sitting in an almost aggressive manner. The first photograph he chose (Photo 2.1c) was of a place in Italy. Mickey said,

> I chose it because I've never been there before . . . I'd like to live out of London, somewhere like Yorkshire'. When I asked, 'but you said at the start of our meeting that you wanted to work in London?', Mickey replied I'm able to drive throughout the night every day . . . there are times when I haven't had sleep for days, so long as I'm able to pop pills, ecstasy, etc.

Dan

Dan was in his early 20s and had a medium build with a pleasant countenance, Caucasian and a slight West Indian accent.

> This photo (Photo 2.1d) seems [like] something not good is going to happen for future or past generation. Someone could pass away or get a shock from bad news. My friend recently got shot. It's like when you see people in news

whose son or daughter has gone missing. It's the area where you are living – this is why I want to try and leave the country.

These vignettes are given as examples of how quickly Photocards can enable clients to say what is on their minds. Indeed, our research (Loewenthal et al. 2015a) revealed that over 92% of prisoners found the therapeutic use of photographs either very helpful (56%) or helpful (36%). But what happens after the client chooses the initial photo?

What happens next?

To answer this question, let's turn to the phototherapy case study of 'Amanda' (this is from my study titled *Talking Pictures Therapy as Brief Therapy in a School Setting*).

As mentioned, Talking Pictures Therapy is an approach whereby photographs are used in brief psychotherapy and counselling with the purpose of enabling clients to express and explore aspects of their lives that they would like to talk about. The next case study of Talking Pictures Therapy is that of Amanda, who was one of four children aged 12 to 13 years old and seen by the author for a research study (Loewenthal 2013a and provided in the next section) in a UK school setting (further detailed case studies of the other children involved can be found in Loewenthal 2013b, and Chapter 11). The use of such photographs will also be discussed, both in relation to working with children and as an approach to brief therapy. In turn, the use of photographs is explored further through the client material with regard to its function as an evaluative measure in assessing the client's 'progress' through the study, as compared with standardised measures of client progress.

Amanda

It was unclear whether Amanda would turn up for her first session of Talking Pictures Therapy. I was told that she had not been to her classes earlier that day; though she did arrive outside the door, she kept moving away and coming back. The special education needs co-ordinator (SENCO) who was passing by asked Amanda to take the gum out of her mouth, but Amanda threw the gum on the floor and rapidly disappeared, followed by the SENCO. When Amanda returned, she rushed into the room and slumped onto a chair. I asked her if she would come and sit on the chair next to the desk where I was sitting, which she did but sat in a way that must have been very awkward for her.

Photographs as process and outcome

When I asked Amanda which photograph called to her, she chose the one of the playing cards (see Photo 2.2a), which featured a joker. The process of going through the cards also seemed to calm her down a little. Amanda said, 'I like to make people laugh, but it gets me into trouble'. She also told me how, four years ago her father died, and that was after her parents had split up. Furthermore, Amanda wasn't told that her father had died and therefore did not go to the funeral. Amanda said that apparently her father's doctor had warned him not to drink because of his lungs and her father had a heart attack.

At our next meeting, Amanda was already standing outside waiting at the start, but it took her about 30 minutes of going away and coming back to come into the room. Eventually, when she did, she rushed in, diving across the room and ending up horizontally across three chairs. Amanda eventually came and sat on the chair next to the desk, but again sat awkwardly, keeping her backpack on, playing with anything she could find on the desk in a fidgety but deliberate way.

I asked Amanda, as in the previous session, to choose a photograph that called to her. When I asked her what she thought the photograph she had chosen was about, she replied 'it's a clearing' (see Photo 2.2b). Amanda then said 'I want to sleep', to which I replied, 'Go ahead'. She moved the cards aside to put her head on the desk and I said, 'You're making a clearing for yourself'.

We then talked about football. Amanda said that she didn't play for the school (though it turned out she did for a Sunday league). When she spoke about not playing for the school team, she did it in a way that seemed to devalue it, but she also sounded as if she really did want to play for the school. I asked her how come she doesn't play for the school and she replied that she wasn't allowed to because she had

Photo 2.2a Amanda's first choice of photograph: 'The joker'

Photo 2.2b Amanda's second choice of photograph: 'The clearing'

previously forgotten to bring her kit for PE. I said, 'I'm not making any promises, but would you like me to speak to the school and tell them you would like to play football for them?' Amanda said, 'Yes'.

At the start of the next session, I was told that Amanda had been suspended the previous Friday for throwing the contents of a soft drink can over the Deputy Head, and as a further consequence she was now in a meeting at the school with her mother but wanted to see me afterward. When she did arrive, Amanda said 'I'm tired' and she took a piece of paper from the desk in an aggressive way and made a concertina.

Amanda then screwed up the piece of paper and threw it on the floor. I asked her if she would put it in the bin. Amanda defiantly replied, 'When I've finished reading' as she took one of the magazines from a side table, but followed this a few seconds later with 'I need to go to the toilet'. I said 'Ok, but first pick up the piece of paper'. As Amanda went out, she picked up the paper she'd thrown on the floor. When she came back, she wandered round the room in an agitated way and started picking at a plastic notice on the wall, saying, 'These could easily break off'. I said, 'Don't do that – you'll get me into trouble'. Amanda stopped and sat down again in the chair next to the desk. We talked about her chances of staying on at school. Amanda said she knew she'd need to show some improvement to stay on. At the end of the session, she said abruptly, 'You will be here next Thursday, won't you?'

At the next session, Amanda still had her bag on her back but was getting easier to talk to. I said it seemed difficult for her to go after the things she wanted and wondered if that's why she played the part of the joker. Amanda didn't say anything, but what I said seemed to reverberate within her. Again, at the end of the penultimate session, she wanted reassurance from me that I would be there the following week for what she knew would be our last session.

In the final session, she sat down in the chair next to the desk without first wandering around, though she still seemed to find it difficult to speak other than in monosyllables. When I asked her once more to choose a photograph that called to her, she straight away said, 'the one of the clearing' (Photo 2.2b). Amanda also told me she had been asked to join the school football team but had said no. At first, the reasons for this did not appear clear, but what eventually came through was that Amanda wanted to train in the week for her Sunday football when the school team met, and that lots of other girls no longer wanted to play with the school team.

I still wondered with her that this might well be the case, but whether it might also be because she found it difficult to go after what she really wanted.

Overview

I think it was important for Amanda to be able to see a man who was supportive but able to hold the boundaries with her. I think she would have particularly benefited from longer-term therapy.

With regard to the before and after evaluations, the PHQ-9 gave a score of 5 at the start of the first session and of 4 at the last session, which indicated a small reduction in mild depression (Figure 2.1, which shows the pre- and post-scores of the

Evaluative measurement tool	Scores	Amanda
GAD-7	Pre	4.5
(Anxiety)	Post	4
PHQ-9	Pre	5
(Depression)	Post	4
CORE-10	Pre	12
	Post	6

Figure 2.1 GAD-7, PHQ-9, and CORE-10 pre- and post-scores

four children; see also Chapter 11). With regard to the GAD-7 representing anxiety, her initial score was 4.5, which reduced to 4, again suggesting slightly reduced mild anxiety. Of particular interest here was the IAPT Phobia Scale where, regarding the extent to which she would now avoid 'certain situations because of a fear of particular objects or activities', this changed from 'always avoided' to between 'would not avoid' and 'slightly avoid'.

With regard to CORE-10, Amanda's score upon the commencement of therapy was 12 and in the final session, 6. This is where 11 or above is regarded as 'the lower boundary of the lower clinical range'. Changes here included that she now felt that she 'often' rather than 'sometimes' felt she had someone to turn to for support when she needed it. Also, Amanda reported that she had less difficulty getting to sleep from 'most to all of the time' to 'sometimes', as well as fewer 'unwanted images or memories distressing her', which moved from 'sometimes' to 'not at all'.

In all, these cases the use of photographs appeared to aid the counselling process but may have also provided something further. As already mentioned in the previous chapter, Martin describes 'photographs provide an unfiltered connection with the unconscious since what takes place within the phototherapy session is rooted in unconscious processes' (Martin 2013, in Loewenthal 2013b).

Working with clients' photographs in one-to-one, group, and reminiscence therapy

Photocards can also be used in many other contexts to help individuals put into words that which can be difficult to express. Such contexts can vary from discussion groups on topics not usually spoken about, from team development (for example, choosing photographs to express first 'where we are now' followed by 'where we would like to be'), to describing the taste of a food, to speaking of a skill deficit (see Chapter 7). However, perhaps the most used approach to working with photos is that of reminiscence therapy (see for overall reviews, for example, Asiret and Kapucu 2015; O'Leary and Barry 2008), where either the person's photos or photos of earlier times are used to explore thoughts and feelings (see Craig 2014; Krauss 2009). This is then where the facilitator actually works with the client's photos rather than Photocards. However, therapeutic work with family albums, where one family member might control the narrative for others, is less prevalent as following the advent of central heating, we now have the digital era with its social media and new forms of found photographs that are now individually controlled.

There are several organisations providing worksheets and assistance here. To give just one example, thephotomanagers.com suggests, once trained (in the case of reminiscence therapy), the following are possible questions one could ask the older person:

- Where was this picture taken?
- Was this your childhood home?
- Who took this photo?
- What do you like about it?
- What do you remember about this time in your life?
- Was this a special occasion?

They point out that all of these are open-ended questions, which can be low-stress and help facilitate storytelling with patience.

Indeed, the client's photos can be used in ordinary counselling, psychotherapy, and psychoanalysis. They can be just talked about or brought into the consulting room. For example, I saw someone who spoke of a large photo in her family's dining room which she said had everyone in it except her. Several years later, towards the end of her therapy, she remarked that she had looked at that photo again – and she was now in it! Again, in my own therapy I decided to show my therapist a photo album I created by choosing one photo from every year of my childhood. Previously, I had had numerous photos jumbled up in boxes, but by choosing just one photo for each of my years, the photos were no longer jumbled up and, to a far greater extent than before, nor was I!

Yet, there is also the danger that we don't treat older persons, let alone someone with dementia, with the civility we might show towards a younger person. I was involved in research on a counselling service established for frail elderly individuals in a UK general hospital (Trethewey-Spurgeon 2004). It turned out that not only was there a demand from these people who had been hospitalised because of a physical problem from, for example, a fall; but that what was often raised were horrendous experiences. These clients for many decades had not had anyone to listen to their too frequently disturbing stories, and it required the employment of experienced therapists who had had their own therapy and supervision.

Conclusion

This chapter has attempted to explore Talking Pictures Therapy and to relate how photographs can enable all client groups, whether they be children, prisoners or the frail and elderly, in brief therapy to speak about their problems. The first examples of prisoners' first responses for why they chose a particular photo are to demonstrate how quickly photos can illicit words that might otherwise never appear or take much longer to emerge. The more detailed cases of young people in schools are followed by quantitative and qualitative evaluations of how helpful photos can be in assisting personal growth.

In turn, this enables a discussion of the use of photographs chosen, and the resulting projection, as an evaluation of client 'progress' made in therapy in comparison with quantitative assessments. Further, it was found that the photographs, in the context of the therapeutic dialogue of the client's projections, may be useful descriptive devices not only for the therapy itself, but also as a form of therapeutic evaluation.

In my experience, and as a rule of thumb, at least two-thirds of counselling/ psychotherapy clients have found such therapeutic use of photographs significantly beneficial, whereas the rest may not have noticed much difference. Very occasionally, it is too much too soon. This was the case when I saw someone at a counselling drop-in centre who couldn't help but choose a photo with what, to most people I think, would look like some innocuous graffiti on a wall. Yet it turned out she had once been sexually abused against a wall with graffiti whilst walking from school. In this case I removed the photos completely and successfully continued the remaining sessions without them.

In conclusion, Talking Pictures Therapy can be helpfully offered to many clients who wish to explore what is really of issue to them in a relatively short time.

References

Asiret, G., and Kapucu, S. (2015). The effect of reminiscence therapy on cognition, depression, and activities of daily living for patients with Alzheimer disease. *Journal of Geriatric Psychiatry and Neurology*, 29(1): 31–37.

Craig, C. (2014). Photography in care homes: Methods for researching practice. In *Sage Research Methods Cases*. www.delloewenthal.com.

Krauss, D. A. (2009). *Phototherapy and Reminiscence with the Elderly: Photo-Reminiscence.* Unpublished paper given at the 2009 International Symposium on PhotoTherapy and Therapeutic Photography, Turku, Finland, 11 June.

Krauss, D. A., and Fryrear, J. L. (eds.). (1983). *Phototherapy in Mental Health*. Springfield, IL: Charles C. Thomas Pub Ltd.

Loewenthal, D. (2011). Researching phototherapy and therapeutic photography. In U. Halkola, T. Koffert, M. Krappola, D. Loewenthal, C. Parrella, and P. Pehunen (eds.), *PhototherapyEurope: Learning and Healing with Phototherapy – A Handbook*, pp. 17–24. Turku, Finland: University of Turku, Publications of the Brahea Centre for Training and Development.

Loewenthal, D. (2013a). Talking pictures therapy as brief therapy in a school setting. *Journal of Creativity In Mental Health*, 8: 21–34.

Loewenthal, D. (ed.). (2013b). *Phototherapy and Therapeutic Photography in a Digital Age*. Hove: Routledge.

Loewenthal, D. et al. (2015). The therapeutic use of photographs in the United Kingdom criminal justice system. *European Journal of Counselling and Psychotherapy*, 17(1): 39–56.

Martin, R. (2013). Inhabiting the image: Photography, therapy and re-enactment photography. In D. Loewenthal (ed.), *Phototherapy and Therapeutic Photography in a Digital Age*, pp. 69–81. Hove: Routledge.

O'Leary, E., and Barry, N. (2008). Reminiscence therapy with older adults. *Journal of Social Work Practice*, 12(2): 159–165.

Rogers, C. R. (1995). *On Becoming a Person*, 2nd edition. Boston: Houghton Mifflin (Trade).

Spinelli, E. (2005). *The Interpreted World: An Introduction to Phenomenological Psychology.* London: Sage.

Trethewey-Spurgeon, C. (2004). *Counselling/Psychotherapy and Older People in Medical Settings.* Unpublished Doctoral thesis, University of Surrey, Guildford.

Weiser, J. (1999). *Phototherapy Techniques: Exploring the Secrets of Personal Snapshots and Family Albums,* 2nd edition. Vancouver: PhotoTherapy Centre Press.

3 Therapeutic photography

Summary

This chapter first focuses on two case studies of therapeutic photography. It provides the photographs for both case studies and a description of the processes undertaken. 'Putting the (m)other first' demonstrates how therapeutic photography can be utilised to work through loss and grief. In this case, the photographs are of the author's childhood home upon the death of his mother. Here, a further question is examined as to whether the photographer is putting himself or his mother first when photographically working through his grief. The second case involves the author coming to terms with, and working through, depression and exhaustion. The chapter concludes with an overview of literature on the increasingly popular field of therapeutic photography.

Key learning points

1. Therapeutic photography is a powerful approach for the activist self-help client, but there are several caveats.
2. There is a real danger that therapeutic photography too easily wrongly becomes phototherapy, whereby clients are involved in making sense of their photographs but without a trained therapist. Instead, it is recommended that therapeutic photography be seen as an activity that can best be done by the self-help activist client by themselves.
3. Therapeutic photography can be conducted by a facilitator, but this requires considerable training/supervision (as with PhotoVoice) to minimise the risk of the client entering the facilitator's often unconscious unexplored minefields.
4. There is a serious problem of premature closure in therapeutic photography (and phototherapy). This is where the use of photographs emotionally moves the person on only to get stuck at a new place.
5. Therapeutic photography can emerge naturally or be planned.

Exercise

Take six photographs, and then write how what you have photographed, or how you have taken the photos, might express how you are currently feeling.

DOI: 10.4324/9781003240914-4

Photo 3.1a 'The blues: 1'   *Photo 3.1b* 'The blues: 2'

Photo 3.1c 'The blues: 3'   *Photo 3.1d* 'Lola'

Photo 3.2a Lola and Lucy

Photo 3.2b Lucy and Lola

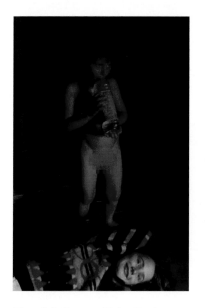

Photo 3.2c Lucy and John-Louis

Photo 3.2d Lucy

Photo 3.3a Jane   *Photo 3.3b* The view from the window

Therapeutic photography: A case of depression and exhaustion

Here are some photographs I took when arriving on holiday with my young family after having worked long hours for some time under stressful conditions. By having a camera to take photographs, I was able to recognise that I was both exhausted and depressed, and this therapeutic photography enabled me to come to terms with this and work it through. I took the first photographs (Photo 3.1) as I lay exhausted in bed. They reflected back to me 'the blues' that I was experiencing.

As time passed, whilst I lay there, my oldest daughter came into vision (Photo 3.1d) and I noticed she was changing and starting to become a woman.

Then, my other children (Photo 3.2) came into the picture, and subsequently my wife (Photo 3.3) and I was once again able to be in the world with others and look out the window (Photo 3.3) again.

One more word of warning: It is important when showing photos to be aware of changing cultural sensibilities. I have now pixelated Photo 3.2c of my then two-year-old son looking very happy and wearing no clothes. Although, when he was older, he did not object to my showing of this photo, I no longer include it in its original form, as subjects such as nude pictures of children can take away from what one is hoping to communicate.

Photo 3.4a Putting the (m)other first
(panel 1 of 7)

Photo 3.4b Putting the (m)other first
(panel 2 of 7)

Photo 3.5a Putting the (m)other first (panel 3 of 7)

Photo 3.5b Putting the (m)other first (panel 4 of 7)

Photo 3.6a Putting the (m)other first (panel 5 of 7)

Photo 3.6b Putting the (m)other first (panel 6 of 7)

Photo 3.7 Putting the (m)other first (panel 7 of 7)

Therapeutic photography: A case of loss and bereavement

The second therapeutic photography project I present here was when I was working through another personal constriction. This was about the death of my mother and the end of the house I had been taken to when I was born and had lived in, on and off, for over 50 years. They were enormous endings for me; I am an only child who didn't have cousins I could meet or much of an extended family. The first time I took the photographs, I was trembling with emotions, and perhaps it's those photos I should be showing (see discussion regarding truth and re-enactment phototherapy in Chapter 5). Instead, I returned with a tripod which led to the photos shown here. As you will see, the overall presentation of 'Putting the (m)other first?' consists of seven panels (Photo 3.4–3.7), each with a large photo accompanied by four smaller ones. I was particularly interested in the extent to which my photos were ethical (see Chapter 10). Ethical, in this case, was defined as the extent to which I was putting my mother first or myself first. I do think the taking of the photos not only helped me work through the loss of my mother and my childhood home but, in so doing, also gave me something of an emotional foundation.

My experience of these two therapeutic photography projects described above for me, both the phrase 'a picture is worth a thousand words' and that photographs can be enabling as 'footprints of the mind' (Weiser 1993 [1999]).

Having provided two therapeutic photography examples of my own work, I will now give an overview of its literature.

So, what is therapeutic photography?

As stated in Chapter 1, therapeutic photography 'often involves self-initiated, photo-based activities conducted by a person, and sometimes without a therapist guiding the experience, for self-exploration and personal growth' (Martin and Spence 1987, 1988; Spence 1986). This can be seen as taking photographs to work through what might be considered an emotional constriction. For example, Jo Spence used therapeutic photography to work through a successful confrontation with breast cancer and an unsuccessful one with leukaemia (Johnson 2016).

Photography can be therapeutic in and of itself; through creating and making, there can be a personal 'working through' that leads to greater potency and potentiality. Photography can also have a societal enhancement effect, for example Hogan (2022: 1) considers '. . . therapeutic photography in its broadest sense, with regard to how photographic practice can aid health and well-being in our society'. Hogan also states that 'therapeutic photography can be where the client is facilitated in the use of photographs for self-development in a way similar to arts therapies' (Hogan 2022: 1). However, my experience is that art therapists, with some notable exceptions such as Wheeler (2013) and Kopytin (2013), tend to use photography in order to demonstrate the stages of other artwork, rather than focussing on photography as a main art form.

Yet again, it is in the act of creating a photograph which leads to a dialectical, elliptical relationship between the photograph and the feelings and experiences of the photographer. This includes the effects of the making and taking of photos on the resulting photographs, as well as the effects of these photographs once more on the feelings and experiences of the photographer.

Furthermore, as with physiognomy, there seems to be something unique about the way a person takes a photograph. I was once on a photography course where we shared a black and white printing process. We almost invariably knew whose photograph it was that came out of the printer, even though we were all photographing the same theme/subject.

More generally, according to Hogan (2022: 2),

> Photography is ubiquitous. The visual image is a predominant form of communication. Arguably it is a very democratic medium, since billions of people all over the planet take photographs on their phones, and digital storage means that expensive printing is not necessary and therefore the practice is not prohibitive. Photography is important to political and social movements and connects people in emotionally meaningful relationships.

There is some similarity for Craig (2009): 'Photography shows us how to look at things from different perspectives, to reflect, to communicate and to express ourselves in a way that goes beyond words'. Craig's focus here, though, is on '. . . how professionals working with groups can use photography to promote self-exploration and positive change'.

Whilst the main developments in therapeutic photography took place particularly in the UK and North America in the 1980s and 1990s, there has more recently been a resurgence of interest, with increasing claims as to what therapeutic photography can achieve.

What is claimed for therapeutic photography?

Here is one particularly interesting claim for the positive benefits of therapeutic photography:

> Therapeutic photography has been shown to be more effective than traditional therapy methods such as cognitive behavioural therapy, psychotherapy or art therapy because it provides an opportunity for the person to experience the world through their lens and see things from different perspectives. This allows them to process their thoughts and feelings in a different way.
>
> Paras (2022)

Who is therapeutic photography for?

As Gibson (2018) states in his well-researched book on therapeutic photography, 'Therapeutic photography is an increasingly popular approach for increasing self-esteem, resilience and self-reliance in a wide range of people, including those with dementia, autism or mental health problems, school children and offenders'.

How does one go about choosing a subject for therapeutic photography?

My examples, given at the start of this chapter, emerged naturally. However, if you are actively seeking what to do, then Mariia Lozhko's (2021) post on Deposit Photos (https://blog.depositphotos.com) suggests five possibilities:

1. 'Respond to annoying thoughts by taking photos'.
2. 'Take selfies daily and show them to others' (this increasingly important cultural field is explored separately in Chapter 9).
3. 'Take pictures of things you feel negative or positive emotions towards'.
4. 'Write stories based on your last snaps'.
5. 'Create your photo map'. This is where you invite others on a photo tour along a familiar route, taking pictures and later drawing a map accompanied by your thoughts from your photos as you travel along.
   Lozhko further suggests that 'therapeutic photography is available to everyone, regardless of their professional level, equipment, and creativity'. I very much agree with this.

PhotoVoice

One of the best-known organisations to use therapeutic photography is Photo-Voice (https://photovoice.org). They state that their 'mission is [to] promote the ethical use of photography for positive social change, through delivering innovative participatory photography projects. By working in partnership with organisations, communities, and individuals worldwide, we will build the skills and capacity of underrepresented or at-risk communities, creating new tools of self-advocacy and communication'.

In answering the question 'Why photography?' PhotoVoice claims,

> A photograph is the quickest and easiest way for somebody to document the realities of their circumstances. Most people are familiar with photography to some degree, and it can be picked up relatively quickly by all abilities and ages.
>
> Photography also crosses cultural and linguistic barriers, with its power lying in its dual role as both a form of creative expression and a way to document facts.
>
> It provides an accessible way to describe realities, communicate perspectives, and raise awareness of social and global issues to different audiences.
>
> Its relatively low cost and ease of dissemination encourages sharing, facilitating dialogue and discussion, even for those who have never picked up a camera before.
>
> (https://photovoice.org/about-us/)

I was commissioned by PhotoVoice to evaluate one of their projects, entitled 'Shutter Release' (Loewenthal and Clarke 2013). This was where PhotoVoice facilitated prisoners to explore issues around release and rehabilitation through photography. The following findings may not be the case for all PhotoVoice projects but may be helpful for those considering using therapeutic photography, particularly in a group or community setting.

The first and most important finding was how well PhotoVoice was able to facilitate the taking photographs without getting therapeutically involved in helping inmates work through what emerged. Whilst such an approach is what is recommended in this book as good therapeutic photography, there was a caveat here in that we recommended that some inmates in the future would benefit from being able to explore what the photos evoked with a separate psychological therapist. This can be needed when, as is so often the case, the initial exploration at first raises, rather than lowers, anxieties. Another finding was that inmates were likely to gain more individually when they took the photographs and less when seeing other inmates' photographs. All workshop participants reported four shared benefits of the process:

1. Increased ability to reflect on their anxieties
2. To be more flexible in their thoughts
3. To think more about the different thoughts of others
4. The ability to think or speak in more depth about their issues concerning release from prison

Planning the therapeutic photography shoot

Therapeutic photography can take place spontaneously; in fact, one of the best photographic approaches I ever learnt was from Peter Fraser (1988). Peter would get his students to have their cameras ready on automatic and then sit in a chosen location for 20 minutes with their eyes closed. Next when the 20 minutes were up, take photos immediately of what they saw. This attempt to not be trapped in a previously learnt frame can provide the most enlivening results, as it appears to connect the camera with one's unconscious. It took me some time to let go, but when I did, the results were always wonderfully fresh. However, the two projects described at the start of this chapter did include considerable planning (once the subject matter emerged). Figure 3.1 provides a template of headings for a therapeutic photoshoot timeline.

	Start date	End date
Preliminary research		
Agreements with interested parties		
Shooting		
Printing		
Editing		
Possible re-shooting		
Possible re-editing		
Deciding and arranging Exhibition/publication		

Figure 3.1 Therapeutic photoshoot timeline

Conclusion

Finally, what could be taken as helpful tips from https://theoneproject.co:

> Use photography for creative expression and introspection to build a solid foundation of healthy habits and tools, release attachment to negative narratives to reconnect with your intuition and build a better picture of mental health for all free of stigma, judgement and fear.
>
> Therapeutic photography involves taking, analysing and using photos for the purpose of personal healing, growth, or understanding, whether done consciously or unconsciously. By actively constructing, exploring and reflecting on photographs by pairing it with creative writing, you are able to learn more about yourself and how you see the world.

I will be showing such pairing of photographs with writing in a variation of therapeutic photography termed 're-enactment phototherapy' in Chapter 5.

References

Craig, C. (2009). *Exploring the Self in Photography*. London: Hachette. https://blog.deposit-photos.com/therapeutic-photography.html.

Fraser, P. (1988). *Two Buckets*. Manchester: Cornerhouse Publications.

Gibson, N. (2018). *Therapeutic Photography: Enhancing Self-Esteem, Self-Efficacy and Resilience*. London: Jessica Kingsley.

Hogan, S. (2022). *Photography*. Bingley: Emerald Publishing.

Johnson, S. (2016). Dust to dust: The photographer who stared death in the face – in pictures. *The Guardian*. https://www.theguardian.com/artanddesign/gallery/2016/feb/16/photographer-jo-spence-the-final-project. Accessed 2 September 2022

Kopytin, A. (2013). Chapter 12, Photography and art therapy. In D. Loewenthal (ed.), *Phototherapy and Therapeutic Photography in a Digital Age*. Hove: Routledge.

Loewenthal, D., and Clarke, D. (2013). *Evaluation of PhotoVoice 'Shutter Release Project'*. London: Research Centre for Therapeutic Education, University of Roehampton.

Lozhko, M. (2021). Exploring therapeutic photography: How you camera and hobby can help you heal. https://blog.depositphotos.com/therapeutic-photography.html.

Martin, R., and Spence, J. (1987). New portraits for old: The use of the camera in therapy. In R. Betterton (ed.), *Looking on: Images of Femininity in the Visual Arts and Media*, pp. 267–279. London: Pandora.

Martin, R., and Spence, J. (1988). Phototherapy: Psychic realism as a healing art? *Ten*, 8(30): 2–10.

The One Project Education Inc. (2021). *The One Project*. https://theoneproject.co (Accessed 2 September 2022).

Paras, J. (2022). *Therapeutic Photography: Exercises in Self Discovery*. Chicago: Independently Published.

PhotoVoice. (2022). *About PhotoVoice – Ethical Photography for Social Change*. https://photovoice.org/about-us/(Accessed 2 September 2022).

Spence, J. (1986). *Putting Myself in the Picture: A Political, Personal and Photographic Autobiography*. London: Camden Press.

Weiser, J. (1993 [1999]). *Phototherapy Techniques: Exploring the Secrets of Personal Snapshots and Family Albums*, 2nd edition. Vancouver: Phototherapy Centre.

Wheeler, M. (2013). Chapter 4, fotos, fones & fantasies. In D. Loewenthal (ed.), *Phototherapy and Therapeutic Photography in a Digital Age*. Hove: Routledge.

4 The creation of therapeutic Photobooks

Summary

This chapter provides case studies of the use of Photobooks as a means of emotional development for individuals and groups. Two forms of creating books using stories are considered. The first, Talking Picture Books, which is explored in depth, is where the client writes a personal book for an actual or imagined person, following the structure provided here. This involves designating a page for each suggested chapter heading and providing each with a chosen photograph and brief description of a thought to accompany. The second type of book, story books, is one where a story is told by selecting a sequence of photographs. The case studies chosen are taken from prison inmates writing these books for their children.

Key learning points

1. Talking Picture Books is a new approach to the therapeutic use of photographs.
2. It has proved to be very popular with clients and psychological therapists.
3. It is again easy to ask clients to choose a photograph and then what thoughts come to them, but it's far more difficult to work with what then evolves.
4. Using Talking Picture Books is different from constructing a story with art work where photographs can also be used.

Exercise

Think of somebody that you would like to send a Photobook to. The case given below (see Photo 4.1) is for a parent to their child, but you can change it to send to anybody – real or imagined. As you will see, the book is structured into various parts. Each part asks you to choose a photograph. This can be done from selecting one from www.delloewenthal.com/phototherapy-and-therapeutic-photography.html. Alternatively, you can choose one of your own photographs or use found photographs (you might even just want to imagine the photographs). Once you have finished, you can either send the book electronically and/or print it off and/or send it to a Photobook publisher. Figure 4.1 provides a template for you to use:

DOI: 10.4324/9781003240914-5

Photobook Template

Figure 4.1 Photobook template

★

This story has been written especially for [name] by his/her [relation], [name], who has selected some photographs with [name] in mind to accompany his/her thoughts . . .

★

Part one: Us in the past

★

This is a picture that comes to mind when I think of you . . .

★

[Insert picture]

★

I chose this photograph because . . .

★

My favourite memory of you is . . .

★

[Insert picture]

I chose this photograph because . . .

★

Part two: About me

★

I want to tell you something about myself:

★

This photograph reminds me of what I like . . .

★

[Insert picture]

★

I have chosen this photograph because . . .

★

And this photograph reminds me of things I don't like . . .

★

[Insert picture]

★

I don't like . . . because . . .

★

Part three: About you

★

This photograph makes me think about what I want you to do . . .

★

[Insert picture]

★

I would like you to . . .

★

And this photograph makes me think of what I don't want you to do . . .

★

[Insert picture]

★

I don't want you to . . .

★

Part four: Us in the future

★

This photograph makes me think about what I am looking forward to regarding you and me in the future . . .

★

[Insert picture]

★

I am looking forward to . . .

Key
★. = new page
. . . = you write here

The following Photo 4.1 is provided as an example of a photobook.

The case of Demario's Talking Picture Books for his son, Nicholas

This book is dedicated to Nicolas

The story has been written especially for Nicolas by his father, Demario, who has selected some photographs with him in mind to accompany his thoughts...

1

Part One

Us in the Past

2

This is a picture that comes to mind when I think of you...

3

4

I chose this photograph because I know you love cars

5

My favourite memory of you is...

6

7

I chose this because it reminds me of when we have been playing football together and you asked me on the phone "when are we going to play football again?"

8

Part Two

About Me

9

Photo 4.1 Example of a Photobook

I want to tell you something about myself:

10

This photograph reminds me of what I like...

11

12

I have chosen this photograph because I like Christmas and it also reminds me of you asking before Christmas to put the presents under the tree so you can open them!

13

And this photograph reminds me of things I don't like...

14

15

I don't like alcohol because alcohol made us be separated. It's not good to drink a lot.

16

Part Three

About You

17

This photograph makes me think about what I want you to do...

18

19

... I would like you to involve yourself in sport

20

And this photograph makes me think of what I don't want you to do...

21

Photo 4.1 (Continued)

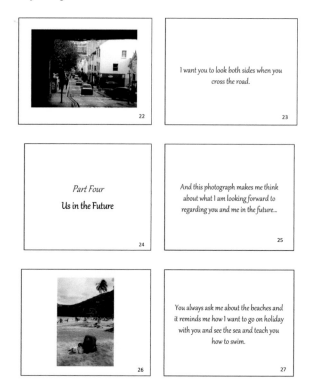

Photo 4.1 (Continued)

In order to give a better example of the book's layout, below is a template, similar to that provided for the exercise, again of Demario's Talking Pictures Book for his son, Nicholas

★

The story has been written especially by Nicholas's father, Demario, who has selected some photographs with Nicholas in mind to accompany his thoughts.

★

Part one: Us in the past

This is a picture that comes to mind when I think of you . . . [Demario chose a photograph of a Mercedes car].

★

I chose this photograph because 'I know you love cars'.

★

My favourite memory of you is . . . [Demario chose an image of some footballs].

★

'*I chose this because it reminds me of when we have been playing football together and you asked me on the phone, "when are we going to play football again?"*'

★

Part two: About me

★

I want to tell you something about myself:

This photograph reminds me of what I like . . . [Demario chose a picture of a Christmas tree].

★

I have chosen this photograph because '*I like Christmas and it also reminds me of you asking before Christmas to put the presents under the tree so you can open them!*'

★

And this photograph reminds me of things I don't like . . . [Demario chose a picture of alcoholic drinks].

★

I don't like '*alcohol because alcohol made us be separated. It's not good to drink a lot*'.

★

Part three: About you

★

This photograph makes me think about what I want you to do . . . [Demario chose a picture of people playing football].

★

I would like you to '*involve yourself in sport*'.

★

And this photograph makes me think of what I don't want you to do . . . [Demario chose a picture of motor traffic].

★

'*I want you to look both sides when you cross the road*'.

★

Part four: Us in the future

★

And this photograph makes me think about what I am looking forward to regarding you and me in the future . . . [Demario chose a picture of a beach].

★

'You always ask me about the beaches, and it reminds me how I want to go on holiday with you and see the sea and teach you how to swim'.

★

Once again, in this method of producing Photobooks, it was the relationship between the facilitator and the inmate that seemed of most importance, as hopefully shown herein in the description of working with Demario on his Photobook.

Describing the process with Demario

I had been told that there was an inmate (whom I shall call Demario) in the mental health block of the prison who had been on constant 24-hour supervision for many months as he wanted to kill himself. I was told that one staff member commented that she had never known anyone so intent on killing himself.

I had also been told that this man had a son that he had not seen for some time, and it was suggested to me that I might help this inmate write a storybook for his son (I had previously carried out what I call 'Photobook Dads' with a small group of inmates at that prison). I was initially concerned that this might be more for the staff to make themselves feel better in that when Demario did kill himself, there would be something from him for his son, which might provide the staff with a better form of closure. I requested that he be asked if he would like someone to work with him in this way. Consequently, I was told that he replied 'yes' and, unbeknownst to the current staff, he also reported that in fact he had received some counselling previously, which he had found useful.

When I first saw Demario, I saw a black African, physically strong and of medium build in his early 30s, sitting and engaging those around him in conversation. He appeared reluctant when I approached him with the occupational therapist to take him to the room for his Talking Picture Books session, which, as I have said, I understood that he had previously reported very much wanting to do. Instead, Demario appeared to ignore us and continued to talk (in English, though clearly this was not his first language) with the other inmates he was with, eventually saying that if he was going to come, he would also want help with his homework from the occupational therapist. As he stood up in a somewhat agitated way, he stopped again and took time extracting some tobacco from one of the inmates he had been talking to.

Soon after, as he finally started to walk with us, he suddenly took a different direction and went up to another inmate demanding tobacco in a way that might have been interpreted as bullying. I intervened, saying somewhat impatiently, 'Look, I've come a long way here just to work with you' (which may also have been interpreted as bullying). After this, he seemed to just follow us.

Upon entering the therapy room, there was a large table with some chairs. I pulled out a chair indicating for him to sit down and then, unusually for me, took a chair alongside him. I asked him about his son, and Demario told me in a quiet voice that his name was Nicholas, and he was now 7 years old. I also outlined the possible chapter headings for the book we were going to create from him to his son and explained how I would be asking Demario to choose various photographs and say something about each for his son. I then asked him if he would help me put the photos out on the table. Demario seemed particularly interested in doing this, so I gave more precise instructions and we communicated with each other as to where the photos should go. For example: 'Shall I put them here?', 'Yes, great', etc. I could sense from the way he moved that he was changing into someone who one could have a good relationship with.

When I asked him the questions which were the chapter headings in the book, I could see that he found it relatively easy to choose the related photographs that came to mind. However, it appeared he could also be easily influenced by what he thought of as my ideas, and I found it important to give him enough space so that he could stand up, albeit he did it very gently/timidly (in contrast to how he had been when I had first met him) for his own thoughts.

Demario was also quick to pick up what I was doing and showed that he eagerly wanted to help me, by, for example, telling me the number on the back of each photograph he chose (without me asking) after I had asked for the first one. One of the first photographs he picked was of some flowers and a small cross at a cliff top where someone had jumped off. I had been told that Demario frequently and determinedly tries to kill himself; he is therefore not allowed any sheets on his bed, etc. He first said of this photo, 'This is a cemetery', but after a little while, he said 'it would not be suitable for my son'. As we talked, what emerged was that it was really his responsibility as a father not to suggest this to his son, and I wondered to myself if it might then have emerged for Demario that he might not suggest it so much to himself. I find that having the possibility of talking about that which most people don't, in this case death and suicide, is perhaps different from much that happens in psychological therapy (regardless of the use of photographs) with the growing influence of positive psychology and its focus on happiness (Layard 2011; Seligman 2011).

When we had finished choosing the photographs and writing down for the book why he had chosen them, Demario said how he gets caught up thinking about his wife and that makes him feel depressed, but now he realises he can think of his son and be happy and have something to look forward to. I said, perhaps a little too flippantly, 'You now have a choice; if you want to feel miserable, you can think of your wife, and if you want to feel happy, you can think of your son'. I added (from my own experience) 'not that sons are always easy'. But I could see that he wanted to speak in a different way and was now finding it easier to do so, so I needed to respond more therapeutically. Demario said, 'I feel guilty that I don't think about my son and that I just think about my problems with my wife'. I reflected this back to him, and what then emerged was more like a conventional therapy session, though without me having started in a conventional way. Demario also told me that he didn't have a photograph of his son and realised he would like one, though he did not need any help in doing this.

When it came to the evaluation form, I asked if he would like to do it on his own or if he would like to fill it in with me. Demario said that he could do it, and with difficulty he read out the questions. As he wrote, he seemed able to ask me at first to spell out the words, and he then asked me if I could write them down, but in a way that felt good for both of us. At the end, Demario thanked me and said how good and important the experience had been for him. His mood seemed to have significantly changed – something had lifted. I felt the same had happened to me, and that I had done something more useful than how I was increasingly in my work 'serving time' (as another type of prisoner).

Subsequently, I learned that Demario was very pleased to receive the book and proudly put it on display. Demario also had acquired a photograph of his son. Soon after, he was transferred to another prison. It was only several months later, in writing this up, that I learned that Demario had been a boy soldier and could not see his son because he couldn't get over the thought that he had killed boys that age.

Describing the Photobook approach

In my workshops, the creation of therapeutic Photobooks is probably the most popular of the five main methods explored regarding the therapeutic use of photographs (as introduced in Chapter 1). This seems true regardless of whether I am conducting them with prison inmates or art therapy students.

The approach described here is the use of Talking Picture Books, which I created initially to develop emotional well-being for inmates in a Category B medium-to-high security male prison in England. In this activity, fathers, either working as a group or individually, choose from the same 52 Talking Picture Cards, as described previously (located at www.delloewenthal.com/phototherapy-and-therapeutic-photography.html; see Photo 1.1), in response to questions devised and posed by the facilitator (in this case, the author). This approach seemed to call to the inmates in a particularly powerful way. Thoughts of their children seemed to link them with the outside world and encourage the development of positive paternal emotions for their children.

Whether in a group or individually, the facilitator gives an outline of the actual hard-covered book that will be produced and briefly describes the different chapters, starting with 'Us in the past'. The facilitator then says, 'With regard to you and your child in the past, please choose a picture that comes to mind when you think of him'. Once the inmate has chosen the photograph, the facilitator asks, 'What made you choose this photograph?' The facilitator then writes down the response and checks with the inmate that this is what he wants as a printed message to his child to accompany the photograph.

This use of Photobooks may be similar to the benefits claimed by the approach used in prison entitled 'Storybook Dads' (Berens and Berry 2013). However, this story book approach involved telling an illustrated, pictorial story (for example, losing and finding a family's pet). Talking Picture Books, in contrast, is structured through photo elicitation for the father to send personal messages to his child.

Thus, Talking Picture Cards can also be used to create a story. I have used them in this way with inmates, enabling them collectively to write a story with the picture cards in a book to be presented to all of their children. This has been found to be helpful in getting them to both enjoy working with each other and gain a feeling of ownership of their creativity. A further therapeutic use of photographs that is related can be in terms of 'tape slide presentations' as outlined in Loewenthal (2013).

Conclusion

As mentioned, Photobooks do appear to provide one of the most effective methods of emotional learning through photography. Asking people to choose a photograph that speaks from them to another is relatively easy. However, as can hopefully be seen with Demario, this can be very involving for the facilitator. Again, in another setting, when a teenager came to 'My favourite memory of you is . . .', she cried, 'but I do not have any favourite memories of my sister' and was then effectively able to explore this. Hence, once more, there is the caveat that, aside from facilitation by a trained therapist, it is best conducted by self-help clients on themselves.

References

Berens, J., and Berry, T. (2013). *Tales from Beyond the Walls: Stories for Children, Written by Prisoners*. Welshpool: Writers in Prison. www.storybookdads.org.uk/.

Layard, R. (2011). *Happiness: Lessons from a New Science*, 2nd edition. London: Penguin Books.

Loewenthal, D. (2013). *Phototherapy and Therapeutic Photography in a Digital Age*. London: Routledge. pp. 117-119.

Seligman, M. E. P. (2011). *Flourish: A Visionary New Understanding of Happiness and Wellbeing*. New York, NY: Free Press. www.delloewenthal.com/phototherapy-and-therapeutic-photography.html.

5 Re-enactment phototherapy

Summary

This chapter explores re-enactment phototherapy primarily by presenting the book I previously wrote for myself describing my father never having recovered from the loss of his parents and sister in the Holocaust, to the extent that he could not talk about his family of birth, nor want anything of value, which partly included myself. Utilising re-enactment phototherapy, I dressed as my father, grandfather, grandmother, and aunt, based on a photograph of each my father originally brought to England together with an extraordinary amount of his mother's Czech crystal. Through this photographic exploration, I started to tell in their voice their story as I imagined it, from when my father left Czechoslovakia to the moment of his, and what was becoming my, family's murder. Already, things were changing. I had never previously called them 'my grandfather, grandmother, and aunt', but rather 'my father's parents and sister'. Now, with trepidation, and through this re-enactment phototherapy, they were becoming 'Eduard', 'Adele', and Hilde'.

Key learning points

1. Re-enactment phototherapy can be a very powerful and helpful tool for working through psychological and social constrictions in one's life.
2. Re-enactment phototherapy can be carried out by the activist client on themselves, with a facilitator therapist, or with a co-worker, where you take it in turns to help each other's re-enactment phototherapy projects.
3. It is strongly recommended that the client has a therapeutically informed, supportive environment.

Exercise

By taking a situation/trauma regarding a past or present: family member or lover or work colleague or friend or classmate, etc. you might begin 'to tell and explore ways of making visible the complexity and contradictions of [y]our own stories, from [y] our points of view, by re-enacting memories and imagining possible futures'. You might consider 'the effects of institutional gazes and attitudes upon [you], rather than seeing these as privatised distress . . . the psychological and social construction of identities' (adapted from Martin (2013: 72).

DOI: 10.4324/9781003240914-6

When undertaking such a re-enactment photography session, write or record your associated thoughts and feelings.

Re-enactment phototherapy: The case of my father, the Kristallnacht Carrier

Re-enactment phototherapy can be seen to be uniquely derived from several traditions (which I have had some involvement with), including psychodrama (Moreno 1946 [2020]), where photography can also be used to record stages of a story, and co-counselling (Heron 1980), where client and counsellor keep changing roles, partly as a means of not structurally creating a power imbalance. I consider re-enactment phototherapy to also be applicable as part of gestalt therapy (Perls et al. 1973), where one can sit on different chairs that represent different voices within oneself.

As Hogan (2022: 143) usefully writes, 'Re-enactment phototherapy is an interesting and powerful practice because of the way it straddles the line between social science research, political activism and art, with a strong therapeutic dimension'. Hogan (2022: 142) quotes Sherlock (2012: 1) in describing Spence's overarching legacy as: 'Taking aim at certain personal and political myths – the family snapshot, the domestic goddess, the cancer victim – her work asks unflinching questions about the power structures of visibility, of who can be seen under whose terms and in what light'.

Yet whilst sometimes clear, for example a strong feeling or a photograph that one keeps returning to, it can be difficult to know where and how to start with re-enactment phototherapy. This is what I wrote at the start of my re-enactment phototherapy journey:

> I will now try and speak what has never been spoken. I will try and write of the experiences of my father, grandfather, grandmother, and aunt. I will accompany these accounts with the only photographs my father brought out of Czechoslovakia of his father, mother, and aunt together with self-portraits of myself dressed in the jacket my father brought to England, so as my father being his father, mother, and sister. It seems important that I speak as my father about what he could not say about his father, mother, and sister, in order that I might be freed up from what the crystals intergenerationally contained: unexpressed sorrow.

This re-enactment phototherapy case study is influenced by the work of Jo Spence (1986) Martin and Spence (1987, 1988), as well as (Dennett 2013) and particularly Martin (2013) (both in Loewenthal 2013b). Various aspects of re-enactment photography have been very influential in various spheres. See, for example, developments in approaches to social change through participatory photography by Winckler (2013) and Winckler and Conway (2006). In the case of 'My father the Kristallnacht Carrier', this form of therapeutic photography was also influenced by the heuristic research of Moustakas (1990) and the post-memory theory of Hirsch (2012) enabling me to bring my relatives alive so I could more appropriately psychologically bury them.

In Chapter 3, it was reported that by pairing photographs 'with creative writing, you are able to learn more about yourself and how you see the world' (The One Project 2020). I hope that what follows illustrates such pairing.

A book within a book

MY FATHER, THE KRISTALLNACHT CARRIER

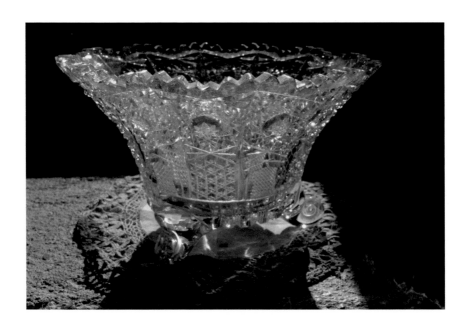

Del Loewenthal

Contents

Acknowledgements

I would like to thank the following people for their collaboration on this project: First, my fellow student, Rainer Eidemülller, and his mum for their thoughts and translating the 50 plus letters I found from old German to modern German and then into English; Gauri Chauhan for her assistance with all things digital; Simon Sandys for helping me to relearn studio work, film developing, Photoshop, and Lightroom; and Liz Nichol for her help in transcribing. My sincere thanks also go to the staff and students of the University of the Arts/London College of Communication MA programme in Documentary Photography and Photojournalism. I also thank my children and particularly my wife Jane who have been there to support and offer insights from the start. However, my greatest collaborators have been Eduard, Adele, and Hilde Loewenthal, together with Grandma Loewy, whom I got to know through what emerged doing re-enactment phototherapy.

The author?

Am I my own author? I, like others, have also been authored by my parents, but, in my case, I am also constricted by what my parents, and particularly my father, could not say. My father's losses were such that I feel I need to work through how they have affected me, including what I have lost as well as gained through this. Both my parents talked a lot, I think in order to not allow thoughts of their own losses to come to them.

To tell the story, at least as I thought it was, when I started this project: My father, Louis Loewenthal, was in France when Hitler invaded Czechoslovakia. He said he was the only person on the train going through Germany, and on arrival, moved his parents, sister, and grandmother from the Sudetenland, which the Germans had invaded, to Lysa, a town to the east of Prague. His grandmother was soon to die there. His father did not want to emigrate and my father after working on building sites, being interrogated by the Nazis, and managing, through a girl he met, to get bogus papers as if he were part of a foreign visiting delegation, left Prague on 1 September 1939. It was in London where he managed to receive an invitation from apparent relatives with the same surname. That night, 1 September 1939, he carried with him a typewriter and an extraordinary amount of his mother's Czech crystal – sweet dishes, fruit bowls, and hors d'oeuvres dishes. On his way, a German soldier in Holland tore up all his papers, and my father said he never knew how he managed to reach England. But he did, arriving with the crystal at a house in London, where the family there had the name Loewenthal and where the person who was to become my mother worked.

My father was subsequently to volunteer for the Czech army and return with D Day allies, eventually reaching Prague only to learn upon arrival of his parents' and sister's murder in Auschwitz and Treblinka. As a consequence, he spent that first night alone in the army camp whilst everyone else was out celebrating.

My father never recovered from this loss, rather he was what might be termed as being 'in denial', such that he could not talk about his family, nor want anything of value, which partly included me. But I still have the crystal.

In writing this, the horrifying thought occurs to me that perhaps I should smash them? But that might be an even more irreparable loss, so I will attempt to work it through photographically.

In thinking about re-enacting my father as he was in 1939, I set about looking for the large blue overcoat that he arrived in and which I had kept. Only gradually did the thought come to me that I had agreed with my wife a couple of months previously that it be thrown away. I then thought I remembered watching from the porch as she put it in the bin whilst she looked at me, ensuring she was doing this with my agreement. This apparent realisation resulted in a tremendous feeling of loss. I thought about the coat's texture and its incredible heaviness that required a sewn in metal chain in order to hang it up. I began to wonder if, unconsciously,

Photo 5.1a The author?   *Photo 5.1b* Crystal 1

Photo 5.1c Crystal 2

Photo 5.1d Crystal 3

finally getting rid of the coat had led to this project. Perhaps whilst I had it, the story could remain powerfully untold. I did wish, though, that I had at least a photograph of it.

Having written the above, my subsequent thoughts included that I needed to do more work photographically regarding the loss of the coat. I was familiar with the idea of re-enactment phototherapy and was becoming increasingly influenced by the work of W. G. Sebald (2018) and, in particular, his use of photographs and text in his story of Austerlitz, where the main character's search for his Czech Jewish roots has some echoes with my own. As I dressed as my father (I still have both his Czech shirt and the jacket that was in his portrait photo), more thoughts again returned to me of his story, which I have previously reported. But now, I was my father, in France, receiving the news of Munich, of Hitler invading the Sudetenland, of being the only person on the train going from Germany to Czechoslovakia, of moving his, now my, parents from Aussig (since 1945 called 'Usti') to Lysa; working on building sites; meeting a girl who got him, now me, appearing to be on the list of a visiting delegation; being interviewed by the Nazis; saying goodbye to his parents and sister (I have only just thought of this for the first time); taking the crystal and his bags and typewriter and getting on the train; having a German soldier tear up all his, now my, papers; arriving in England, somehow, at the Loewenthal (no real relation, but there appeared to be no help offered from my father's large extended family who had already safely left) house in Ealing; and meeting the owner's daughters, both of whom were a similar age to my father, and the person working there who was to be my mother. Getting work in England, volunteering for the Czech forces in England and travelling with them around England and Scotland, getting married, going with the D-Day forces to invade France and head back through devastated Germany to Prague, being the only one in that army camp on the first night when everyone else was celebrating, and learning that his, now my, parents and sister have been killed. Finding an apartment for my mother to come and live in Czechoslovakia, having to escape again when it is clear the Russians are not leaving, going back to England and looking for work, advertising to try and find his, now my, sister, spending the rest of his, now my, life in denial and trying to avoid anything of value, whether it be books, a house, a car, a child, or acknowledging a wife's qualities, that could be taken away. (Is this why I am also critical of those I am close to – not so much as a Jewish characteristic but rather a safeguard against loss, even if it is unfair and cruel to others? Perhaps it's also related to my problem of not throwing things away because when I do, I frequently throw away what I want to keep?)

I next thought of dressing as my father's mother, father, and sister (I still do not say my 'grandfather, grandmother, and aunt') and telling the story again from their points of view. It is this that, understandably, I think my father could not bear to do and that I need to do for him, though it is really for me. I also wondered about telling the story, as in Seebold's Austerlitz, but going through it again from my father's point of view, then my grandfather telling the story, then my grandmother telling the story and then, probably most difficult, my aunt telling the story. I thought that I need only symbolise

Photo 5.2a Crystal 4

Photo 5.2b Crystal 5

being these members of my family – I am saying 'of my family' for the first time in my life – by wearing a different shirt as my grandfather and a blouse as my grandmother and I'm not sure what as my aunt; she is the most difficult to wonder about.

Over the next few days, I found myself thinking about my family's actual names, instead of saying my father's family: My grandfather 'Eduard', my grandmother 'Adele' (it might have been eerie for my father that my friend's nicknamed me a similar sounding 'Del'), and my aunt, 'Hilde'. I also wondered if all this was leading to a rapprochement with all things German. My father had refused to speak German since that day when he learnt of his father, mother, and sister's deaths, and whilst I wasn't aware of any personal antipathy to German people, I had avoided buying German goods when there was a choice. Now, a few days later, when depressed because the UK was leaving the EU, I found myself wondering if I could get a German passport! In researching this project, I read that the Sudeten Germans had been given German nationality after Hitler invaded and I thought maybe that had happened to my family – only later thinking 'but not for Jews'. Yet this wanting a German passport, almost more than a Czech one, was such a turn around. Whilst not being Jewish myself (my mother was Church of England/Chapel, having been born in London's East Ham, but was brought up in South Wales and hence had a Welsh accent), I had always identified with Czech German-speaking Jews. Particularly Franz Kafka; Edmund Husserl for philosophy; Sigmund Freud, who was born there, for psychoanalysis; Mahler (and Dvorak) for music; even Robert Maxwell for Jewish stereotyping; and, more recently, the playwright Tom Stoppard. I was interested in equivalent German figures: Hannah Ahrendt, the Frankfurt School, Max Scheler, Kurt Weill, Albert Einstein, even Leo Loewenthal, but I didn't identify with them. I also was proud of such Czech statesmen as Thomas Masaryk and Vaclav Havel.

I had always dreaded when a new acquaintance would say 'that's an unusual name – where does it come from?' I would defensively reply that my father was from Czechoslovakia and that he, his father, his grandfather, and his great grandfather were born in Bohemia. Telling someone I was getting to know my surname and getting a response of 'what a pity' symbolised my own experience of not being accepted. Regarding my father's caution to volunteer that he was Jewish, there was some family evidence for this, as my mother's sister had not allowed my father in her house because of his German name – we had been at what was a war with them. So, as you will see in the following stories, history repeats itself: If one didn't get persecuted by the Germans, one got persecuted for appearing to be German! But was it more than 'appearing to be'?

I again thought about how I had to get over the loss of the blue coat. I wondered about filming or photographing it, as I had imagined I'd seen going into the rubbish bin. But then, the next week, my wife phoned me when I was at work, very excited to tell me that it had not been thrown away but instead put in a pile of items to be disposed. So, can I rely on my own memory? And what to photograph now? Perhaps the typewriter and coat should be part of an exhibition, but dare I put the crystal in the exhibition, let alone all of them, without something catastrophic happening?

The following week, after having been up late, I took the photos of myself wearing my father's jacket but wearing different shirts and ties and then blouses under the jacket as if I was my father being his father, his mother, and his sister. When taking the photograph, I was not particularly emotional; however, soon after, I thought again of naming the photographs not as 'my father', 'my father's father', 'my father's mother', 'my father's sister' as I have always done but as 'my father', 'my grandfather', 'my grandmother', and 'my aunt'. Soon after, I then thought of naming the photos with first names: 'Louis', 'Eduard', 'Adele', and 'Hilde'. And several days later, I thought of putting my first name, but not just as Del, which my friends had nicknamed me, but as 'Derek', the name my parents gave me.

Some days later, I remembered that when I was a boy, I had asked my father with some trepidation why he had not anglicised our surname (I suspect I wanted to have a go at him). He replied, 'because my parents died for it'. This had a profound effect on me, partly perhaps because he had never spoken of his family. I thought it was a very good answer and didn't question it again. But now, today, for the first time, I felt I could have anglicised my name and had a much easier time as a result. In contrast, I had only recently requested that my eldest daughter put my surname as part of our first grandchild's name. Also, I now keep thinking how it seems so important to me that I was wearing my father's jacket in the original re-enactment photographs. It was as if he had to remember his parents and sister in order for me to be released from his loss. It was important that I speak as my father about what he could not say about his father, mother, and sister, such that I might be freed up and become more my own author.

A further memory kept coming and going like a fog. It was when I was a young boy and one Sunday I dressed up in black and went to where my father was sitting – I can remember the place exactly now – and I got his attention and did a 'Heil Hitler!' salute in front of him. He was very angry, but again nothing more was said. I had wanted a reaction – a filling of the gap of what was not said.

By now, I had phoned the German embassy and asked if they thought I was eligible for German citizenship. All this personal movement has come through, freeing up what the crystals contained: Unexpressed sorrow.

I will now try and speak what has never been spoken. I will try and write of the experiences of my father, grandfather, grandmother, and aunt. I will accompany these accounts with the only photographs my father had of his father, mother, and sister, together with photographs of the crystal.

I think my father had known that his parents and sister had been forced to move to an apartment in a restricted area of Prague. But he did not know what had happened to them until, through volunteering to join the Czech army, he was part of the Allied forces triumphantly returning to Prague to hear only then of their murder in Polish concentration camps. From that moment, it would appear that my father could not accept the news. My mother told me initially how my father would pay for newspaper advertisements in search of his sister. In fact, it was only in 1969, when my father met me at the airport, that I immediately confronted him with the news that I had seen all three of their death certificates through relatives I had discovered, despite my father not giving any information about them, in North America. At that moment (when I was 21), my father was, for the first time, noticeably unable to respond. Prior to this, the subject was such a 'no- go' area, and it could not be acknowledged even that it was a 'no-go' area. Indeed, I again remembered, with some guilt, an occasion when I was around twelve years old dressing completely in black and approaching my father who, as ever, was reading the newspaper (he would read it every day literally from start to finish as well as watch every news programme – perhaps it was a way of not allowing thoughts to come to him). But now the fog is lifting and I can see clearly, what I could previously only briefly mention on that Sunday afternoon, the green armchair he was sitting in next to the dining room window and I went right up in front of the newspaper and shouted, 'Heil Hitler' whilst simultaneously giving a Nazi salute with one hand and the forefinger with the other hand signifying a moustache. I remember my father reacting angrily, but I cannot recall him saying anything, which I had probably unconsciously hoped.

It would appear from that moment in 1945, when he was on his own in the army camp after hearing of the death of parents and sister while all others were in Prague celebrating, he was a broken man. He did not want anything of value, I think for fear of losing it; he no longer wanted to have books, he did not want to own a house (we always lived in perilously leased accommodation until my mother managed to put her hand up to buy our house in an auction in 1973). My father also did not want to claim his professional qualifications or equivalent English ones when he had the opportunity, and, according to my mother, he did not want children – I was a mistake! Whilst in some way it was clear that my father loved me very much, in other ways he didn't want me to succeed for fear of losing something of value.

I have a very vivid memory of a particular moment of saying goodbye when we walked together, as was often the case, I on my way to school and him to work. On this occasion, I was about to sit my eleven plus exam. As we were about to part, my father's last words to me were, 'What will you do if you fail?' I took this as a confusing message to attempt to fail, which haunted me for much of my life in that I also find it difficult to do things that I really want to do, and I am forever throwing away things I really want without knowing I am doing it at the time. Sometime later, I did confront my father as to why he said that to me when I was about to take such an important, life-deciding exam. His reply to me was, 'Can't I speak to you as an adult?'

I have put a question mark after 'The author' at the start of this chapter. In order to be more freed up, I felt I had to get my father to speak of his parents and sister so I might be able to speak and think of them as my grandparents and aunt, which I had never been able to do. I do remember, when burying my father in April 1986, that the thought came to me as if from nowhere, 'At last, his sister has been buried'. However, this couldn't happen then, as first she would at least have had to have appeared in my family narratives. I therefore thought I would have to be first my father as his father, then his mother, then his sister, with each of them telling the stories, however briefly, that couldn't be told.

My father, the Kristallnacht Carrier

What follows is my father's account of events that led him to leave Czechoslovakia. It was written ostensibly in order to help retrieve money that his mother had deposited on his behalf in a Czech bank, though the first draft of his letter, which is reproduced here, may also have served as a way of partially working through the trauma of his loss.

In the matter of the Czechoslovakia
(Settlement of financial claims)
Order 1940 and the Statutory Declarations
Act 1835.

I, Louis Loewenthal of 3, Cherry-tree-Avenue, Yiewsley
in the County of Middlesex do solemnly and sincerely declare
as follows:

Having finished the Commercial Academy at Usti
n.L.(Bohemia) I started to work at the firm I.Petschek,Usti
n.L.on the 14 th of August 1930 and stayed in its employment
to the end of September 1938. The firm I.Petschek, Usti n.L.
has been one fo the biggest mine-owner and wholesalers of
coal in Central-Europe, including Germany. After working for
one year in different departments ,I started in the department
for import of coal from Polish and German-Silesia to Czechoslovakia. After a short time I had to deal with the correspondence. In 1935 two clerks of the Department for North-and
Nortwest-Bohemia went into retirement and their department
and the department for import were combined and I had to deal
with their correspondence as well.1938 I spent my holidays in
France with the intension of get away fomm any political dis-
cussions, but the alarming and contradictory news in the French
newspapers influenced me to cancel my holidays in order to be
home if war should break out. I took this as certain. On the
night of Godesberg I passed the German-Czechoslovakian frontier
and a day after I went to my firm offering my services,because
many had been already called au to the colours; others had left
for security. I had no military training. At this time I lived
at 122, Masaryk-street at Usti nad Labem. My father (70 years

Photo 5.3 My father's account of events that led him to leave Czechoslovakia page 1 of 6

- 2 -

of age at this time), my mother and grandmother (80 years of
age) went to Prague to my sister when riots had broken out
at the time before Goderberg. When war with Germany semmed
certain they went to Lysa n.L. but without any furniture. I
tried to get the furniture away from Usti n.L., which would
have been in the fighting zone, but I could not arrange trans-
port. At the time of Munich I remaindd the only one at the
office, who had anyting to fear from an Hitler-Regime. Luckily I met Mr.Petschek and he advised me to go to Prague and to
report there to the managing director. I madethe suggestion
of taking documents and typewriters with me, but Mr.Petschek
declined and asked me to leave as quickly as possible. When
I came home, I found unexpectedly a lorry waiting, which I
tried to hire before. I packed whatever I could get on it and
left Usti n.L. on the 30 th of September 1938 in the evening
for Lysa n.L. Next morning my parents and I had to go to the
Town-Hall in Lysa n.L. and we were told to leave Lysa n.L.
within ten minutes to return to Usti n.L. (Sudetenland), that
meant to Hitler. We could understand the excitement and bad
feeling of the police and people in the rest of Czechoslovakia,
but we have been the worst victims of the Munich tragedy. We
were able to stay in Lysa, after providing a doctor's certifi-
cate about my grandmother's ill-health and proving that I intended to hold out to the last minute I came especially back
from France. In the meantime I heard from my firm that they
would employ me again, if they should recommence business. I
did not want to stay idle and as I had the intention to go
abroad - keeping in mind that I would not have much chance to
get the essential permission to work in Czechoslovakia, as I

Photo 5.4 My father's account of events that led him to leave Czechoslovakia page 2 of 6

-3.

have received in the meantime a second expulsion-order from the
Prague Police to leave Czechoslovakia for Sudetenland. I intended
to do manual work and made use of an old acquaintenceship with
an architect in Prague, who got me a job with a building-firm and
there I worked for about two weeks as a mason. Owing to new works-
regulations the builder had to dismiss me, but luckily my old
firm started again and asked me to come there. The firm I.Petschek
fought hard to get permission to re-establish itself in Prague;
the laws and regulations were on its side, but the German „political influence and pressure was too big. The application was refused.

In the meantime all refugees from the Sudeten-district
had to fill in different forms and as we feared that the Germans m:
might ask later on for money, my parents and I mentioned only a
small amount. In November 1938 Germany and Czechoslovakia came
to an agreement about the refugee-question and it was then obvious
that any village or town would refuse to give the right to stay
there, (if the person was to become perhaps a burden later on to
the town or village. It was therefore advisable to bank your money
where you wanted to get your citizenship. I asked therefore my
mother to bank my savings of   Kc. 15.000.-
in Lysa n.L., which was carried out in November/December 1938.
on my name only. I came home from Prague (I lived till 8./XI.38
at Prague I, Rybna 11 and since then at Prague I, Josefovska 4)
almost every weekend and returned to Prague every Sunday night.
I do not know the exact name of the Savings-bank, but so far as
I can remember from a discussion with my mother, there existed
only one bank; it is situated in the main street, near the town-
square on the right hand side, coming from the railway-station.

Photo 5.5 My father's account of events that led him to leave Czechoslovakia page 3 of 6

-4-

I believe its name is: Mestaka Sporitelna, Lysa nad Labem.
It seems great carelesness on my part, but I knew my savings-book
was quite safe in my mother's hand. The fight for existence was
very strenuous and hectic at this time. In the meantime my application for a permit to work had been refused; but my firm had made
application for a new one through the mine-owner's federation, but
without any success. Some time after my firm was refused permission
to establish itself in Prague. The situation for my firm looked
very hopeless. The Germans - the mines were in their hand - delivere
90% of the output only to the Zivnostenska banka. In view of the
state of affairs at the end of February 1939 our worksmanager decided to pay us an annuity. All employees got at least one year's
salary; I received   Kc.30.000.-
representing about eighteen months salary. It was very generous
gesture. At the following weekend I gave the full amount to my
mother to bank it, which she did.
        Since about November 1938 I have tried to immigrate
overseas, but without any success. On the 14th of March 1939 I
wrote to four of my namesakes in London and four in New-York to
give me any assistance to get out of Czechoslovakia. On the 15th
of March 1939 the Nazis marched into Prague unexpectedly. The savings
account stood at Kc.45.000.- at the 14th of March 1939.
        On the 18th of March 1939 I received a letter from
Mr.Theodore Loewenthal, 58, Hanger Lane, Ealing, W.5, inviting me
to come to him. I was very pleased and thought to have found someone
in England, willing to give me a hand for settling my affairs with
any oversea-country. When I heard next morning from the managing-
director of our previous establishment in Vienna that he was travelling to England at the invitation of an English friend of his, I
went at once to the British Consul. I was told there, that the lette

Photo 5.6 My father's account of events that led him to leave Czechoslovakia page 4 of 6

-5-

Mr.T.Loewenthal would be sufficient, but I must hurry because fro
the 1st of April 1939 a British visa would be necessary. All
banks were closed from the 15th of March 1939.and it was not possible to get any foreign exchange for the purpose of buying the
fare. With very good luck I overcame all the difficulties of getting the permission from the Gestapo for leaving Czechoslovakia
and the fare. To equip myself the necessities I asked my mother
to give me   Kc.1.000.-,
which she surely withdrew from my savings-book, when the banks
reoened again. I left Prague on the 27 th of March 1939 and I
gave my mother, Adela Loewenthal, nee Loewy and my sister,
Hilda Loewenthal power of attorney in all affairs. My ticket was
via Venlo. The Dutch authorities would not let me pass there
without British visa and advised me to go to Oldenzaal, where a
British Committee had been installated. I had to travel through
the Rhineland to Oldenzaal without any ticket, because I had not
enough money on me. Mr.Loewenthal in Ealing, hearing that I was
stopped, gave guarantee for me and I could land in England on the
1st of April 1939. Mr.Loewenthal gave me hospitality and I lived
at his house 58, Hanger Lane, Ealing W.5 till the 30 th of September 1939. At the Czech Committee in London I heard later on
that the Hicem-Committee in Prague considered my case favourably
as being under danger of Nazi, resp.Fascist persecution and put
me me on its list for emmigration to England. Unluckily they
could not inform me in time owing to the events of the 15 th of
March. The guarantee, generously given by Mr.Loewenthal in
Ealing , prevented my getting any financial assistance from the
Czech Committee (I got altogether for two weeks ten Shillings
pocket-money). I did not like to accept any money from Mr.Loewen-
thal, although he offered me several times; I gave some German

Photo 5.7 My father's account of events that led him to leave Czechoslovakia page 5 of 6

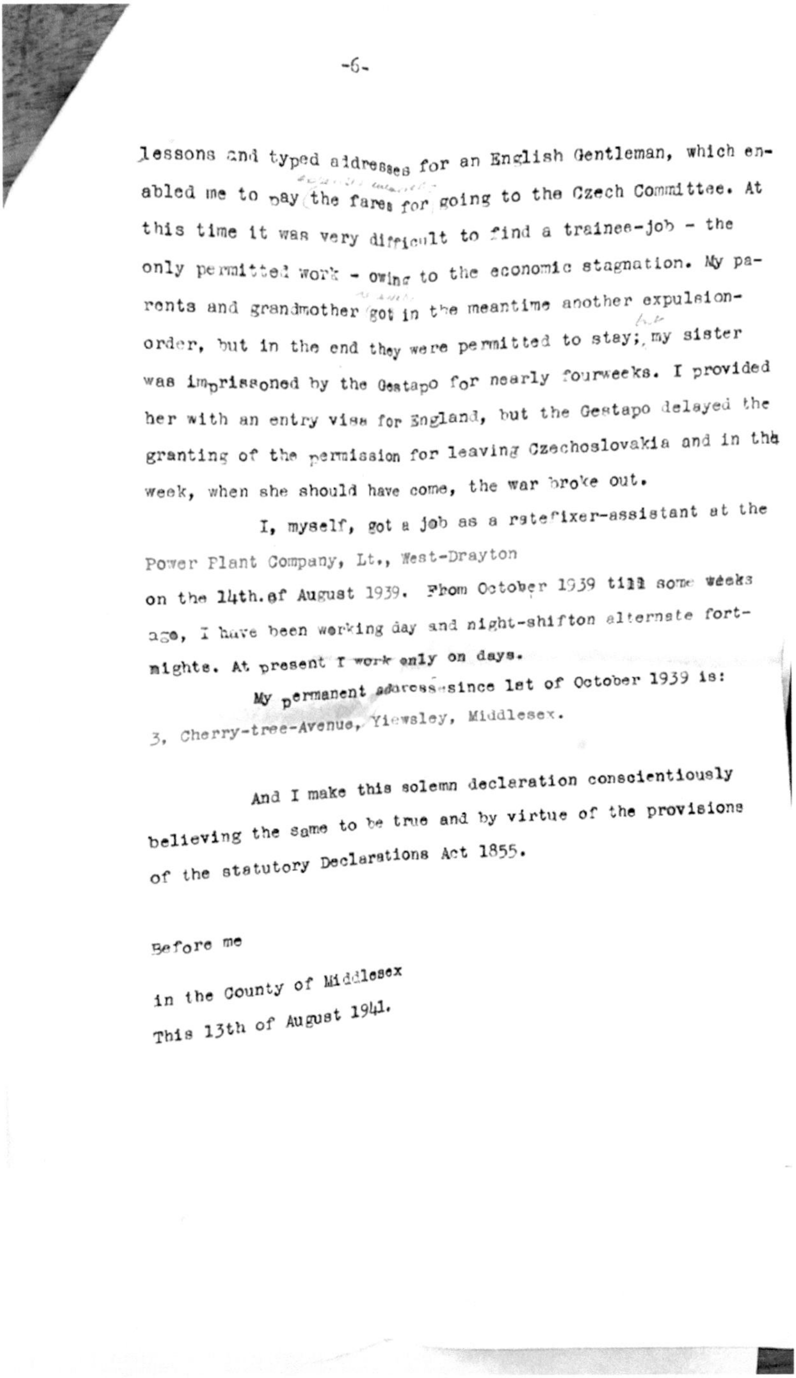

-6-

lessons and typed addresses for an English Gentleman, which enabled me to pay the fares for going to the Czech Committee. At this time it was very difficult to find a trainee-job - the only permitted work - owing to the economic stagnation. My parents and grandmother got in the meantime another expulsion-order, but in the end they were permitted to stay;.my sister was imprissoned by the Gestapo for nearly fourweeks. I provided her with an entry visa for England, but the Gestapo delayed the granting of the permission for leaving Czechoslovakia and in the week, when she should have come, the war broke out.

I, myself, got a job as a ratefixer-assistant at the Power Plant Company, Lt., West-Drayton on the 14th.of August 1939. From October 1939 till some weeks ago, I have been working day and night-shifton alternate fortnights. At present I work only on days.

My permanent address since 1st of October 1939 is: 3, Cherry-tree-Avenue, Yiewsley, Middlesex.

And I make this solemn decleration conscientiously believing the same to be true and by virtue of the provisions of the statutory Declarations Act 1855.

Before me

in the County of Middlesex
This 13th of August 1941.

Photo 5.8 My father's account of events that led him to leave Czechoslovakia page 6 of 6

Eduard

My name is Eduard Loewenthal. I, like my father before me, was born in Bohemia, but was brought up in Regensburg with my seven brothers and sisters, which was a particularly big family given that my parents, as Jews, had to wait many years before being given permission by the German state to marry. I know my father Jozef was alive until he was over 90 years old, and the same was true of my mother Marie. I also had expectations of a long life. My father was a successful importer of food, having major contracts to supply the Kaiser's army. I attempted the same business, though I was not so successful. Later in life, I married Adele Loewy, who is much younger than me, and we moved to an area called 'the Sudetenland' in what is now Czechoslovakia but was then part of the Austro-Hungarian Empire. If you look at a map today, you can see that there is a train line that runs on the German side of the mountains surrounding Czechoslovakia from Regensburg through to Dresden and over the border to what was then called Tetschen and its smaller twin town on the river Elbe, then called Bodenbach (now called 'Decin' and 'Podmokly' respectively), where we lived. Here, my children were born, Louis in 1911, and our daughter Hilde two years later.

It is said that I want to spend too much time in the coffee shops reading newspapers and discussing current affairs. Yet, I am sure that all the potential horrors that the others speak of will not come to pass and that we will be able to continue our lives here in relative peace. I say this despite what others say, including my son, who I fear is influencing members of my family against me. But that has always been a strange and strained relationship. Why was it when he was very young that he ran away from home on more than one occasion, including once being found in a distant part of Czechoslovakia having somehow got himself on a train? Perhaps that is what happens when a young boy is surrounded by an adoring, perhaps too adoring mother, her mother, and my beloved Hilde, his sister. I have heard it said that when my son brought a girlfriend home, she found us as a rather strange and unusual family, whereas, as a younger boy his friends seemed always fascinated by the different seeds and other items which I was importing and had samples of in my bureau.

It therefore came to me as a massive shock when the British signed away the Sudetenland at Munich in 1938 and, with it, let the French off the hook with regard to our mutual treaty. The Czech army was so strong and well-equipped, and the natural fortifications of the mountains encompassing the north of the Sudetenland and all of Czechoslovakia would have provided, with some help from the French or the English, a good chance of resisting any attempt by the Germans to advance on us. Furthermore, we Czechs were more than willing to fight! But now, my son has returned from his holiday in France and is organising for us to immediately leave our home. We can only take what we can carry out of the Sudetenland, south to our daughter in Prague and then to Lysa in the east. This time with increasing race riots and withdrawal of our rights; all German speaking Czechs who are not Jews have been given German nationality.

I have to agree to go, though I still would like to think things will work out. Yet when we arrive in Lysa, we now have so little, and my wife's mother is increasingly unwell. The people of Lysa do not want us either. They say that we are German and have caused the invasion of their country! But where can we go that is home? Finally, but only because they can see that my wife's mother is dying, they allow us to stay (we can stay if we die!). Also, my son has managed to bring some of our furniture out and he sees us at weekends supporting us from his job with Petschek in Prague, although it is unsure how long this will last as Jewish businesses are increasingly forbidden. Then, my wife's mother dies and is buried in Lysa's Jewish Cemetery, and my family makes friends with a Catholic family who have so kindly helped us with this. Soon after, all Jews are ordered to live in a particular area of Prague and we are forced to go there, with Germany now having invaded all of Czechoslovakia. By now, my son is desperately pleading with us to attempt to leave. He is writing to my relatives whom I once helped and have now lost touch with, all of whom have left for countries beyond Europe to South America, North America, and Africa. I keep forgetting, how could I, but my beloved Hilde was one day arrested by the Nazis who kept her for a month. We don't know what happened; none of us talk about it, and we are just glad she is back with us.

Now we are the only ones of my extended family left and I can see the worry is taking its toll on my dear wife, Adele, and yet I still think that by staying we will be alright in the end. It will not be as bad as some people make out; as a family, we have survived persecution for centuries, so why not this time? However, my son has now found some people in England who will pretend he is a relative and besides his typewriter, his best suit, and his overcoat he is taking with him much of the crystal that his mother holds dear, which we managed to bring from Bordenbach to here. All the other good china he has packed in a large tea chest and has left in the basement of a friend's house in Prague. I see him go off carrying all those heavy weights to a new world like so many of my family members, and I look forward to when we can all be together again when all this has blown over. At least my beloved, beautiful daughter Hilde seems to agree with what I am saying and is staying to look after us.

Yet, having had to leave Lysa and made to live in a ghetto in Prague because we are Jews, we are now being told we must leave Prague for a new destination. It turns out to be Terezin, central Czechoslovakia, where we are forced to sleep on tiered wooden large bunks, twenty to thirty on each tier. However, there is some wonderful music and for a time, things start to improve, but it turns out this is because the International Red Cross is visiting, and once they leave, our existence quickly deteriorates again. Life is intolerable here, but I still have my wife Adele by my side and sometimes I see our loving daughter Hilde, who was also made to come here.

Then, one day, we are taken to the railway and forced into cattle trucks without any food or water, let alone sanitation, for what seems days. Finally,

Photo 5.9a Crystal 6

Photo 5.9b Three crystals

we arrive at Auschwitz. By this time, I can hardly feel or think other than my head being filled with the screams of those dying around me and feeling my own aches and pains and the soreness from my soiled clothes. Eventually, the train stops, and the cattle door is loudly opened – the light is blinding, even though my eyes are closed. I get out with great difficulty; there is music playing. It's as if we are being welcomed. As we arrive inside the gate, I am my wife are asked to go to the right. Hilde was still in Terezin; she was not sent with us. I notice we are with all the old people; the younger ones were sent off to the left. Now we are told that we must first of all have showers and must take all our clothes off, including rings, and leave them with anything else we have brought. This is very humiliating, and I feel so exhausted. And yet one can only meekly obey.

Yet maybe it is necessary for us to be clean so that life can get better. But now we are being forced into one large chamber packed in so closely I do not know how one can have a shower? The door closes, and as it does, I see my beautiful, faithful Adele with watering eyes as she holds me whilst there is the sound of new air being forced into the chamber. But it has a smell of gas and I start choking and gasping with my loving Adele and all the others. I can't believe this is happening.

Adele

My name is Adele Loewenthalova. I was born in Bohemia. My maiden name is Loewy, and it is said that I come from a very good family. I would also like my family to practise more of my faith, but my dear husband Eduard will have very little or none of it. We brought up our family with my dearest son Louis being born two years before my wonderful daughter Hilde in Bordenbach, which was part of the Austro-Hungarian Empire. Then, after World War I and seven years after the birth of Louis, it became Czechoslovakia – though that was not to stay. In Bordenbach, we lived in a modest apartment, and my husband's food importing business was not always good, but we were able to have a maid whose rolled-out bed would be in the kitchen.

My son, after leaving commercial college, got a good job with the Jewish-owned firm Petschek, which has coal mines in Silesia, and my strong-headed daughter, Hilde, works for a Trade Union in Prague. Bordenbach and its larger twin town on the Elbe, Decin, have many political factions. I do not want to get involved, but they worry me. We have experienced so many pogroms. Then, when my son was on holiday in France, the British Prime Minister signed us away in September 1938, permitting Germany to annex the Sudetenland from Czechoslovakia. It was only weeks later, that November, when there was the Night of the Broken Krystal, Kristallnacht, when the windows of Jewish-owned stores, homes, and synagogues were smashed by paramilitary forces and German civilians with the German authorities looking on. We were later to find out that this was the start, with thousands of Jewish men being sent to concentration camps and many Jewish people murdered that night. But my husband says these things happened before and then went away, and so I hope he is right, but I can't stop worrying. But now, my son has returned and tells us we have to move from the Sudetenland immediately. By now, my husband very reluctantly agrees, and I see that we must, although I worry about my mother's health.

We arrive in Lysa, east of Prague, but the people say we are German Czechs who asked Hitler to save them from what they claim, very wrongly, was their persecution and say we cannot stay there. We try and explain that, far from being us who did the persecuting, we are the persecuted ones and, as a family, have very much identified ourselves as German-speaking Czechs and not as Germans. We have come to their town to flee Hitler's policies. But it is to no avail, and they tell us to go. Then my dear mother, who could not bear the upheaval and for whom none of us can bear to think what all this must be like at her age, becomes critically ill and, as a result, the authorities in Lysa allow us to stay. Soon after, my son arrives. He has somehow managed to find a lorry to bring our furniture to Lysa, where we had been living very primitively. The furniture makes us feel a little more at home, but my mother continues to deteriorate and soon she passes away. She is buried in the small Jewish cemetery (which later, unknown to me thank God, is destroyed and replaced by the later Communists with garages, but my son returns just before he dies to erect a stone in memory of her and all the others who are buried there).

By now, we are allowed to stay in Lysa, even though my mother is dead, and our son comes to see us on weekends from his work in Prague. Hitler has not kept his word; he is not satisfied with just the Sudetenland as he promised he would be. He is now in Czechoslovakia and takes over the whole country. I hear from my relatives that his Gauleiter has taken over as his residence the house of my cousin in Prague (what a compliment!), and we are now being forced to live with the other Jews in a ghetto area of our capital. It all gets much worse; my son can no longer work at Petschek, as it is a Jewish firm and therefore cannot exist. They gave him more than a year's salary, which I put in a bank for him, but now he gets some work on building sites – a very different kind of work for him. He wants us all to leave Czechoslovakia immediately, but still my husband wants us to stay; he says it can't get any worse. Louis, my son, has written to relatives who left Europe several years ago at the start of the troubles, but they do not help despite what my husband did for them, and in particular for the family of his brother when he died. However, my son is determined as usual, and he has written to other people with our surname. One of them, Mr Theodore Loewenthal, from a place called 'Ealing' in London, has replied, and somehow, my son – I think through another one of those girls – has gotten himself onto a list of foreign delegates visiting Prague, which he hopes to use to leave the country. I spend time writing lists of people we know, or have heard of, who might be able to help him, as he now can only take two English pounds with him, and I do not know what he will do for work. Louis also takes most of the fine china that was from my family for safe storage with a friend in Prague, but he takes with him to England my crystal, which he knows I hold as dear as I do him. What a weight, though, for him to carry along with his typewriter and knapsack. He looks so smart, like he always does, as he leaves with his fine suit and large, dark blue overcoat. At least that will keep him warm as the winter is soon to come; I can see, though, how difficult it is for him to leave us. I cannot put into words what it means for me to see him go. Yet I am pleased that at least he is going, regardless of whatever happens to Eduard and myself. I do hope our daughter Hilde can join him soon, even though she says she wants to stay to look after us.

Later I get a letter – perhaps he wrote many that I did not receive. Louis tells me that he is safe, and that Theodore Loewenthal lives with his wife in a large, beautiful house. He has two daughters, and my son has also met the family housekeeper, Muriel, a girl his age who was brought up in South Wales and moved with her family from London when she was four years old. It looks like he is very much in love with her, and he does not mention his previous girlfriend.

Meanwhile, Hilde is taking a cooking course, which Louis thinks will help her get to England. At last, Louis manages to raise the money to get Hilde the papers to leave. But the very day she arrives at the border, the barrier stays down, and they no longer allow any Jews to leave. Hilde had for so long put everything into going after countless rejections, never giving up. Now, while she tries not to show it, I know she is devastated. Then we are told to each pack a small bag, and the three of us are made to take a train with only Jews on it. We do not know where it is going. It turns out to be Terezin. Eduard and I are separated from Hilde, and we are made to sleep on very large, tiered bunk beds, about thirty of us on each tier. It feels intolerable, yet the Jewish community, when it can, attempts to organise for a better life and sometimes, I don't know how, there are amazing concerts which give us momentary relief. Also, for a short while, things improve and the Germans organise sports events, but then, when what turns out to be Red Cross visitors leave, things get even worse.

Then one day, Eduard and I are herded not onto an ordinary train, as when we arrived, but as cattle into a cattle truck, those that are slow are savagely beaten. This must be the end, and where is my beloved Hilde – she is not with us – but at least she is not with us. I do not know how long we are in that cattle truck, but we are packed like sardines; it is dark other than occasional chinks of light, people are crying, and we have nothing to eat or drink and nowhere to excuse ourselves other than to mess the clothes we are standing in. The smell of our own and others' defecation is all we have to eat, and I think some of us are already dead, but how else can this journey end? How long does it take for a cattle train to go what turned out to be out of Czechoslovakia, through the length of Germany into Poland – it seemed never-ending, but Eduard and I were still alive when the train finally stopped and the doors opened. It was so very difficult for us to move again, let alone to carry our small cases with what we had left of what was precious to us, as we attempted to get down from the railway carriage and walk with dignity despite our severe lack of food and water and having to walk with our soiled clothes with whatever falling out down our legs. Eduard can hardly see, and we don't try to look at each other. But now things seem to change. There is a sign saying 'Welcome' and a small orchestra playing such sweet music. We are told we must first have showers to prepare us for the new lives ahead, and I notice how many of us older people are made to form a separate queue from the other ones. We are told to take off all our clothes and leave them and all our bags in a separate room. It is still humiliating to be naked in front of other people, but my hunger, thirst, and worry are greater concerns.

Those of us who attempt to keep something are violently handled, so no one else dares to do the same. We are again packed into a chamber even tighter than the cattle truck. How would the shower work – we have not been given soap. I can see that the water could come out of those holes in the ceiling, but now the door is closed. There is no light. Rather than water, I hear the sound of gas and smell it! Some people scream but it is too late. I can no longer breathe, but at least I am with Eduard, and whilst I worry where Hilde is, the one thing that means everything to me is that at least Louis is safe.

Hilde

My name is Hilde. I was born on 7 December 1912 in Bordenbach, which was then part of the Austro-Hungarian Empire. War was to break out two years later, and four years after its end, where we live became part of the new state of Czech-oslovakia. Whilst we speak German at home and Czech outside of it, my parents and at least their parents were born in what has for so long been Bohemia. And this is where I was born and spent most of my youth. I have a wonderful family; my father is a little eccentric, some think lazy because he spends time in the cof-fee shops reading the newspapers and arguing about everything, but I don't think so – for me, he is adorable. My mother, while she comes from a well-to-do fam-ily, is very protective and caring, yet sometimes worries too much. Her mother lives with us; she keeps us all together and I love to hear her play the zither. My wonderful brother, Louis, doesn't always seem to get on with father, but all three of us women think there is little he can do wrong, though he can sometimes be a little too determined! Yet I love him so much, perhaps all the more for it. Like my brother, who is active in the Jewish youth movement, I want to make a difference to the world and as soon as I could work, I got a job on the staff of a trade union in Prague. When I was turning twenty-five, everything got a lot worse for me, and to nearly all the other Czechs' profound horror and dismay, British Prime Minister Chamberlain gave away the Sudetenland to Hitler under the false hope that it was all Hitler wanted and that there would then be 'peace in our time', but the reverse happened. It was so terrible to hear that, for Chamberlain, it was only 'a quarrel in a faraway country between people of whom we know noth-ing', because, we Czechs were militarily strong and the mountains that surround Czechoslovakia, including the Sudetenland, provide natural fortifications; once Hitler was let in, those natural fortifications are no more. Why can't they see that we have military strength and the motivation to fight for our country? Yes, there are German speaking Czechs who are fascists and are very active in our town, but I do not think they are the majority. Our problem in the country is that whilst we do not wish to be occupied by the Germans, we do not wish to invite in the Russians, who are willing to fight with us. As with the Russians, we do have a similar joint treaty with the French requiring them to automatically fight with us if we are invaded. We relied on this and saw the treaty as unconditional, but the

French, in a very underhand way, got out of this by saying that Chamberlain, the British Prime Minister, is representing them. However, our Czech Prime Minister is right: If we allow the Russians in, then they will never leave.

Soon after Munich, where the British Prime Minister Chamberlain sold out to Hitler claiming 'peace in our time', there is the Night of the Broken Glass (Krystallnacht). We later hear not only of Jewish synagogues and businesses being smashed, but of Jews being killed and rounded up by paramilitary fascists while the so-called 'authorities' just look on. I am very worried, as is the rest of my family, except for my father, who thinks it will all pass over. Maybe he is right, but he is also older and hopes that there will not be a dramatic change. He is seventy now, whereas my mother is only in her fifties and is very worried. I do not share my concerns with her and instead try and reassure her that Papa is probably right, but suddenly, the world changes very fast. Still, my parents and grandmother do agree to come and have a holiday with me where I am now living in Prague and away from the tensions in the area of the family home near the German/Sudetenland border.

My brother Louis, who has been on holiday in France, on hearing the news returns on a train through Germany to us. He tells me he is the only one on the train. Perhaps it would have been better, given what he thinks will happen, for him to have stayed in France but that is not like him. Louis says that we must leave the Sudetenland immediately and that there is not time to lose. He is so determinedly convinced of this that my father goes along with the rest of the family, who take less convincing given the increased level of discrimination and abuse we are experiencing. My brother tells us to pack essential or valuable items that we can carry on the train to Prague and then another train to Lysa, which is nearly an hour's journey east of Prague. We hope that what we have left in our apartment will be safe, but nevertheless, my brother organises for my mother's fine china to be packed in a tea chest and kept in the basement of his friend's house in Prague. However, the glass, mainly crystal, which is so very precious to my mother, he hopes to carry for her to London. It is such a weight and I don't know how he manages, but there is no question of him not doing this, such is the love of my brother for his mother.

There is one person I haven't mentioned who is in all our minds. We cannot think what she is going through – it is too much for us. This person is my grandmother; she is very seriously ill, but we and she know we have to move, and I so hope that what my father says is true, that all this will pass over and things will get better soon.

Yet what we first face in Lysa seems even worse. The community there decided we are representative of the German Czechs who invited Hitler to invade the Sudetenland, so they tell us to go back from where we came. However, by now, my grandmother is dying I think; she could not take the move and all the upheaval, and the people in Lysa can see that she cannot be moved again and allow us to stay. My grandmother has been through so much; we shouldn't have moved her, yet without her, we would have had nowhere to go. So, her subsequent death overwhelms us with grief, but we cannot dwell on it too much, perhaps because we feel guilty for what we did to her, particularly as it turned out to be to our advantage, and also because our world continues to change in such frightening ways, and we cannot stay thinking for long about anything else.

Photo 5.10a Me as my father, Louis

Photo 5.10b Me as my grandfather, Eduard

Photo 5.10c Me as my aunt, Hilde

Photo 5.10d Me as my grandmother, Adele

We have rented some very basic accommodations, but miraculously, my brother suddenly turns up with a lorry and most of our furniture from Aussig (the next town down the Elbe from Bodenbach, where we all moved to once my brother got employment there). I don't know how he did it, but he has! Also, whilst we have lost my grandmother, the people of Lysa no longer call on us to leave. Some have become friends. My brother and I continue to work in Prague, but then Hitler invades the rest of Czechoslovakia, and no Jewish businesses are allowed to continue. My brother's firm pays him over a year's salary, which he gives my mother and I to

Photo 5.11a Louis Loewenthal

Photo 5.11b Eduard Loewenthal

Photo 5.11c Hilde Loewenthal

Photo 5.11d Adele Loewenthal

bank for him here in Lysa. But very soon afterwards, we are told that all Jews must live in a restricted area in Prague. My brother now finds us an apartment there. Soon after, the Germans come to where I work and take me to what we call the Nazi HQ. I am held there for a month without being able to tell any of my family where I am. They must be worried sick. When I am let out, nobody really asks me what happened, and I don't tell them; I'm not going to tell you now.

My brother says our only hope is for us all to leave Czechoslovakia and continental Europe, as all our relatives have done a long time ago. However, my father still does not want to leave, and I feel I must stay and look after my parents. But now my brother, with a heavy heart, is determined to leave and hopes the rest of us will follow – he has written to relatives, but no one really helps, even though we know that in the past, my father has helped many. I wonder what it is about us that makes them want to forget us? My brother Louis has now taken to writing to people with the same surname as us, hoping they will realise our plight and say we are relatives. Louis finds this so difficult, for he does not like asking for help and I think he is often awkward in the way he does it – because of this, it doesn't help him. Now he tells me a Mr Theodore Loewenthal from a place called 'Ealing' in London has written to him offering to help, but how will my brother be able to leave Czechoslovakia? Yet he is determined. He has managed to work as casual labour on building sites to bring in money for us, and now I think through a girl he has met he has managed to get his name on a trade delegation from Prague. So, he will appear to leave with them, though he still, as with everyone else, is only allowed to leave with what amounts to two British pounds. I cannot bear to see him leave, yet I am also pleased and proud that he is managing this. When we say goodbye at the station, we are all crying; he looks so smart in his fine suit and big blue overcoat. He has taken his knapsack and along with his typewriter, he has taken my mother's crystal with some other red glass and china, all very precious to her and therefore to him. How though will he ever be able to carry it on his journey? How will he ever get it through Germany and whatever other German-occupied countries – Holland, France – in order to get to England? I hope he is going to be alright and that one day I can, I will, see him again.

Now we have received a letter. Louis has arrived in England. He writes that he doesn't know how he managed it – all his papers were torn up by a German soldier who made him get out of the train in Holland, but somehow he managed to then travel without having these or a railway ticket. He also tells us that whilst Mr Theodore Loewenthal has two very nice daughters. there is a girl there who works as a housekeeper called Muriel who he gets on with very well. She and I were both born in 1912, but she in a place in London called 'East Ham', though he tells me she has a fascinating Welsh accent, her family having moved there when she was four.

Louis tells me that every day he tries to raise the money required for me to join him. He thinks I might be able to get work there as a cook, and on his instructions, I immediately do an intensive course in cooking to get my diploma. He also keeps all our mother's crystals in his room there. I wonder though if he isn't missing his library of books that mean so much to him and to us. Then, after so many rejections for so long, the day arrives when he eventually, somehow, finds the money and I finally obtain the correct papers. I must now do what I have said I would never do and say goodbye to our parents. I hope not for long, but I don't even want to say that to our beloved parents, as I am at last on that train to join my brother. When the train gets to the border with Germany, I am not treated well, but after so many years, I am used to it. I am also twenty-six years old and know how to look after myself, but hope my anger doesn't show. But this time something else is happening.

The German guards say that from today the situation has changed and no one like me is allowed to leave Czechoslovakia. I feel broken and resigned as I return to my parents and to our apartment in Prague, where we then continue to exist for almost three years. Then, in July 1942, we are told on very short notice to go to the railway station. We are only allowed the clothes we are in and a small suitcase. I go with my parents and sit with other Jews in a crowded railway carriage, but we do all have seats, and after a couple of hours, we end up in a town in Czechoslovakia called 'Terezin'. This is totally different from how it was in Prague. We sleep twenty/thirty to a bunk in tiers. I am very active with others in trying to make the best of what we have here. We even have our own orchestra, yet everything is so ominous. I also have to be extra vigilant because people say I am attractive and sometimes, though not often, it is not only the Nazis who are the aggressors.

It is still 1942, and more Jewish people are being brought to Terezin; it looks like others are no longer with us. I see my parents as often as I can, though they are made to live in another part of the camp. Then, one week in October, I do not see them anywhere and I hear they have been taken away by train. I do hope I can join them soon and make sure they are alright. In fact, I managed to get myself near the area of the camp where I think people are being transported from and yes, I am being made to leave, but this time it's so different. It's not a passenger train – it's a cattle wagon, and we are being forced into it like sardines. Somebody about my age (I am nearly thirty) starts to protest but is violently struck down, and we all unwillingly continue to walk past him. Some of the others in the cattle wagon look as if all hope has finally gone from them. They are still quiet until the cattle wagon is violently closed and locked. There is hardly any light and it is difficult to breathe, and now some people start to sob while others pray. We are like this for many hours, if not days, before the carriage comes to its final halt. Some of my fellow passengers have died. The rest of us who are still alive are so thirsty and hungry and our clothes are soiled with our own excrement. I still try and keep my dignity but not to show it too much, for this will only invite an immediate, fatal reprisal, but there appears a strange welcome for us. Here there is a band playing, and I learn that we are in Poland in a place called Treblinka. I do hope I will now meet my dear parents. As we enter through the gates I, with other young people, are made to turn left whilst older people have to turn right. We are all told to leave our belongings in one pile; how will we find them again? Then, we are told we are going to go on a walk so that we can get some exercise, but as we continue, those that do not or cannot march are violently clubbed to death and still we march. By now, several hours later, I am one of the very few left, but I have not eaten or drunk for days now, and my feet hurt so much in what is left of the shoes that my dear mother made for me out of nothing that I cannot go on for much longer. I am starting to stumble even more and realise that it is very unlikely that my parents are still alive. At last, I will be joining them, and there is one thought going around in my head that for so long, through all of this, has kept me going: 'At least Louis and the crystal are safe'. That is it. I am collapsing, I can no longer go on, my knees and my head hit the ground and, for a moment, I feel mother Earth in this foreign land against my whole body and then such violent, too violent, pain.

The grandmother and all those people who are not remembered

To return to what is hopefully becoming more my voice as author: My father, Louis, did not bring a photo of his grandmother, and I now realise I had forgotten her. I do though think she was very important to him. When my father knew that he was coming to the end of his life, he returned to Czechoslovakia, where he placed a memorial stone to his grandmother and all those who had been buried in what had been the Jewish cemetery in Lysa. He also put up a plaque to his parents, sister, and other relatives (whose cemetery had been destroyed) in the new Jewish cemetery in Prague – where I proudly noted that Kafka is buried.

Photo 5.12a Photo of my great grandmother and all those people who are not remembered

End Peace

I am still left with the question as to why my father took all that crystal with him when he first escaped. That Bohemian hand-cut glass must have been so heavy and difficult to carry. Yet he managed to bring with him even more of his mother's china: Figurines, a china cup, and some delicate red Czech glass. Why did he bring them? It may have been that his mother wanted him to. It may have been because it was thought he could sell them, as he was not allowed to take other valuables with him. I think, though, that he simply loved his mother so much. This is again all speculation, but what I do know is that my father left a large tea chest containing his mother's china in the basement of a friend's house in Prague before he left. Sometime after the war, this friend wrote to my father

Photo 5.12b Letters found in the attic

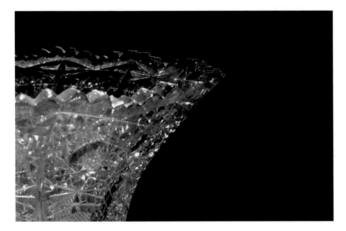

Photo 5.12c Crystal

Photo 5.12d Attempted burial

in London saying that he still safely had the chest and its contents. My father replied, 'Keep it, or give it away', for by now much of the life force was absent from him – it seemed like he feared that anything he desired, including me, would be taken away.

Yet just as I am concluding telling the stories of my father's family that my father couldn't tell, I go into the loft and find an old suitcase. In it are my parents' papers and within them, I discover letters sent to my father in England from Eduard, Adele, Hilde, and Großmama (grandmother). This is amazing. My father must have known they were there, but never mentioned this. Now, after over 70 years, I might hear my family's actual voices. The letters are so precious, I can hardly touch them. The thought comes to me that perhaps when they are translated (it turns out they are in old German and will first have to be translated to modern German and then English), I will be able to bury them, and all can rest in peace. Soon after this, I feel terrible as I cannot find them; they are not where I thought I had safely put them.

But somehow, I manage to find them again – I know I would not have lost them if they were not so precious to me.

Re-enactment phototherapy after discovering the letters

Hearing the letters being translated was an extraordinary experience. Already seeing each family member's handwriting and signature gave each of them character, but now to hear their words was riveting in what emerged – it was like, but more than, excitement, though now with anxiety that I had experienced when, as a young boy, I saw white photographic paper giving way to specific images.

A very close, loving family emerged, and it took time for a steady state to appear of the everyday pleasantries becoming repetitive, though tinged with a reluctant communication of the monotony of their lives. It was during this time that I decided to retake the re-enactment photographs in a studio that I had initially taken quickly with an iPad (see Photos 9.2 and 9.3). This time it was different; I didn't experience the excited anxiety I had when I first did this six months previously – the photos then showed how hyped up, scared, and manic I was. This time I thought of myself more easily as Eduard, Adele, Louis, and Hilde Loewenthal.

What I found, somewhat to my surprise initially, was how relatively easy it was for me to identify with Eduard and how I looked like Adele. This might be because I am similar in age now to Eduard then. I said to myself,

> I am Eduard Loewenthal, son of Joseph and (I had to think for a moment) Marie, who are buried in Regensburg where Joseph had his business (as a supplier of provisions, including for the Kaiser's army). I have many brothers and sisters, including my sister Caroline, and people say I am poetic.

This last point is new from the letters, and I stop myself from allowing thoughts as if they are Eduard's that have come from my previous email re-enactment fantasies.

I felt relatively little when I prepared to be my father's mother, Adele Loewenthal (how strange, I thought, that I ended being called a similar name – 'Del'). The impression from the few lines of the letters so far translated is that she was the practical one of the family. She was the one who wrote out international business addresses for my father. What I did notice was how easy it was for me to look like her without trying too much. There are clear traces of her bloodline, but I don't even know the name of her mother and father. This is partly due to the patriarchal system we are born into and partly my resistance to familiarising myself with what I have never named as family.

To my surprise, the ones I identified with least were my father and his sister, my aunt. Perhaps this is because, whilst I was able to get into some sense of youthful determination and confidence, it was still at least partially overshadowed by my experience of my father as he was not before but after the murder of his parents and sister. I am very aware of using the word 'murder'.

The clothes I wore to represent Hilde worked well, but I found it difficult to embody them. Again, this may be that for most people, it is easier when older people are killed than young ones. However, I think it is compounded by my father being unable to speak of someone who was almost too important to him. What I did feel throughout by attempt to be all four of my family members (I was going to say 'relatives', but perhaps this is the first time I have thought of them as 'family') was that they were very close and whilst not very well off, they were very educated, through probably a combination of schools, self-education, and private lessons. I was reminded of Hilde's letter speaking of how monotonous life was from the time they escaped to Lysa. I assume this was in contrast to the relatively intellectual life they led in the Bohemian Sudetenland. (My father had been an accountant but spoke, to varying levels, seven languages and had been proud of his library that included books by Schiller, Freud, and Jung; he had an interest in Shakespearean plays and the music of Wagner and Chopin as well as Dvorak). As I write more, I become even more aware that in attempting to be my father telling the story, previously untold, of his family, I am increasingly able to tell my own – and about time too!

However, each time I touch the letters I feel anxious. Soon I hope to have more translations which will bring these people even more into my world, but for the moment, the untranslated letters, though touched and written on, seem so fragile. Also, once I take them from the suitcase, there is a real fear that I will lose them. I do think I have unconsciously taken the message from my father to get rid of that which is valuable and precious to me. Further, when I'm in the process of shooting photographs, hopefully of a better quality than when I first started, as me, as my father, and then as my father's parents and sister, I realise with a growing panic that I have lost the original photos. This is very similar to many situations, including when I thought that I had agreed for my father's overcoat to be thrown away. This, as has been noted, turned out not to be the case, and hopefully this may be true with those photos that are so valuable to me.

My life-long anguish is such that it continued to paralyse me so that I am reluctant to throw anything away or even remove photographs on a film card that

I have downloaded. Too often I have selected that which I want to keep and have thrown it away, as, for example, happened with my precious photo transparencies. Hopefully through this work I may one day find this easier, but for now, if anything, it feels worse. I am not quite in no-mans-land, but I am now waiting for more translations having spent time numbering and photographing the letters to be sent for translation (here it would have been better for me to arrange them where I can in a chronological order, but such logical rationality is still too much for me at the moment). Sorting through my father's papers looking for such letters is difficult enough.

After the letters: Crystal clearer

The magic starts to go. The effect of listening to the recording of more letters enabled my extended family to appear in their ordinariness and closeness. As a result, I started to be able to lift and touch the crystal in a different way. I actually washed all the crystal and re-photographed it. Being able to now handle the crystals also went alongside being judgmental – marvelling at some aspects and finding others ugly. They were also different now to photograph in that I did this with more ordinary feelings. There were no longer accompanying emotions of unvoiced, unspeakable anxieties. The project was becoming less important; in other words, it was starting to work!

Even my name, especially my name, seems to have a different relationship to myself. I remembered yet again when, as a young boy, I had asked my father with then unclear, guilty intention why he had not anglicised our surname, and him replying on that one rare occasion 'because my parents died for it' (I don't think he could bring himself to include his sister or grandmother).

Later, upon reading the transcripts of the oral translations, I once again got caught up in that special heightened, confused, and charged sense of excitement and sadness, horror, and yearning. However, this now came and went and reminded me of a bereavement process where one comes eventually to terms with one's loss. This is perhaps what was happening?

From the letters, I also learnt how what I thought had been certain was not in my account of my family's lives and deaths. For example, I had thought my father had carried his typewriter with the crystals when he left Prague, but it turned out that the typewriter had been sent to him by his family after he arrived in England. I first went to correct the initial personal accounts I had created but then realised the importance the stories had held and left them as they had been. What then came to life was that other ornaments my father had also brought with him from Czechoslovakia, which were much more delicate than the crystals, started to come to mind and I photographed them. These included a figurine and some Bohemian red glass.

What might I now say in light of the letters about these members of my family, including my great grandmother, who had previously not been in the picture? But now, the thought occurs to me that she wasn't there because she might have been even more important to my father than his sister. However, this is to speculate again, and instead I would now like to write of these family members based on the evidence in the letters.

To start with my great grandmother – she is still a blank screen in that I have no photo and no name, but the blank is now much smaller. The longest letter I have from her is the following:

> *My Dear Louis*
>
> *Today I'm the first to write to you. I was happy to read the letters you addressed to me, especially that you're well off and healthy and, thank God, I can also tell you that everyone here is healthy. Mum is totally occupied. Therefore, I'm cooking by myself and I'm happy that I can do what I want. Aunt Feny received a letter. She wants to send her daughter on a one hour train ride to school. She will go back and forth daily. Here around our place there was nothing for her to do, no kids with whom she could play. Feny can stay in her flat but she needs to have another woman move in. Her pension has continued and as long as she received it she can stay. Did you answer the letter from Walther? If not please write to him. The weather is not very nice. Either it's very hot and this week it's rained since Sunday and it's really cold.*
>
> *Always be kissed by your loving Grandmother. Many greetings and best wishes to family Loewenthal for the engagement.*

She seems practical and she speaks of my father writing to her. Also, I found that Hilde had written to my father asking him to send back his socks from England for her to darn. The family did seem to love her (as indeed they did each other), as I think is shown by the letters to my father which follow, starting with her son-in-law, my grandfather Eduard, on her death.

Eduard was someone I found, to my surprise, that I identified with. Not only was he similar in age to me now (I ridiculously imagine myself to be in my late twenties, like my father and sister were, then rather than seventy!) but I found myself wanting to identify with him. As my fellow student Rainer said in translating into English from the new German, which Rainer's mum had previously translated from old German, 'there was something poetic about him'. Eduard also had a sense of humour when writing about, for example, appearing lazy for staying in bed so long because of the cold, etc. His beseeching my father to dress warmly and look after his health reminds me of my father speaking similarly and often adding when addressing me 'your health is the number one!'. I fear, as their son and grandson, I could have done more to attempt to instil this in my children. I also was struck how in my grandfather's letters he would always address my father affectionately, signing off 'with deep kisses', as in the following letter:

> *My Dearest,*
>
> *A shiny meteor has come down to earth. We handed our beloved head of family, the creator of the Earth went back. You can be very proud to be the declared darling of the passed away. Every time she talked of you her eyes were sparkling and still in her last moments she thought of her Louisler with love. Thank her for that by thinking of her in your lonesome hours. She carried the crown of thorns of life with pride and steadfast belief in God and when we sum up her life we can say all in all she was a woman we will not see one of her kind any more. Keep her remembrance.*
>
> *Be deeply kissed by your father, Papa*

The photo (5.12d) of my grandmother, Adele, is mocked, again affectionately, by my father's sister Hilde (my aunt) when she speaks of her mother looking like a boarding school matron. Again, Adele, like her mother comes across as a very practical person, though here as elsewhere, I get the impression that however much my father wrote, his mother Adele would complain he wasn't writing enough!

My Dear Boy,

We are waiting daily to receive a message from you, unfortunately without getting one. I hope you're well and for sure occupied. Unfortunately, I have to give you the sad message that we buried our dear grandmother on Thursday the 8th at 3pm. As tender and good as she lived, her death was the same. On Sunday afternoon, she said she didn't feel well. I called for the doctor who told me it's just the flu. On Monday, she said if my Louisler would know how ill his grandmother is. In the afternoon, she still sang a song for Hilde. Tuesday morning around 7 she was not able to speak any more and around 9:30 she died in my arms. She didn't know that it was coming to an end. Please pray for her on Friday evening if it's possible for you. She was so religious.

Frieda and Willi were with us.

Be deeply kissed by your loving Mum

Whilst I wanted to identify more with the mischievous look in Eduard, as in my grandfather's photograph, it was my re-enactment photograph of my grandmother that, I use cropped as my own portrait.

It is Hilde who, with her youthful vitality, is still the most difficult to write and think about. This is what she wrote to my father, her brother, on the death of their grandmother:

You can for sure imagine how we feel. She was lively until almost the end and on Sunday she still read the newspaper and followed all events with great interest. Monday afternoon she still sang so nice:

'When I will die two maidens will play the zither all the time because I can't be sad with all the love I carry in me'

With all of that she was still in a very good mood. Neither she nor us would have believed that was the last afternoon we spent together so we can all comfort ourselves that she had a beautiful life because we all tried to fulfil her every wish and to keep all stones out of her way and so she left the world as tender as she was all her life.

My dear brother, I will soon write more. Now for today, kisses from your Hilde

I though was so moved by the following story Hilde wrote of the two flies:

I always come up with the story of the two flies who fall in the pot of milk. One killed herself in the instant but the second one started treading in her fight for survival and she got ground below her feet as an island of butter was created and she could reach the rescuing shore. I want to be the second fly and by speeding up I want to try to remain on the surface. Hilde 15 April 1940

It is her *joie de vivre*, her playfulness, as she says to her brother how she misses arguing with him, and also the affection with which Eduard and Adele refer to her as 'the little one' that makes hearing of her continued struggle to be that fly that doesn't give up the more difficult to hear – so understandably unthinkable for my father.

And what of my father, Louis Loewenthal? He showed such persistent energy in his attempts to free his sister. I found replies – all negative – from embassies, consulates, refugee agencies in South America, North America, and Europe. I did feel sorry for him with his family's persistent demand for letters – twice a week was not a lot for them! Yet I knew regardless my father did not like writing letters, but it looks like he did then and it seemed to mean so much, almost everything, to his parents, sister, and grandmother.

And what of me? I think I am more my own author. When I was about nineteen years of age, I wrote a poem (which, on reflection, may have come to mind in wanting to be associated with my grandfather):

> *Slipping but not stripping graciously along*
> *Off that balance, that balance that I have kept for so long*
> *Onwards yet downwards to the depth of beyond*
> *Where nothing lies and nothing is wrong*
> *Now I don't exist except in a heavenly bliss*

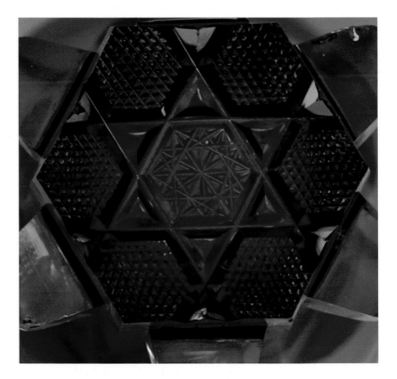

Photo 5.13 Star of David found on underside of Czech crystal

> *But still doubts about love*
> *Doubts of my name.*

I still have 'doubts of my name' in that yesterday, some people I was hoping to get on with – and I think was starting to – asked for my email, and in giving my name I felt that familiar unwanted feeling of being rejected by gentiles, Jews, and even those who repeat 'not to mention the Germans'. Yet I do own who I am more. I also realise my heritage from Adele Loewy's family for the first time and have chosen as my portrait a close-up of the one I took as her.

My father brought me so much, and I have no doubt that he loved me, but as the Kristallnacht carrier, he also brought me much inter-generational trauma. At last, I can understand now his inability to tell the stories, which have for the first time now been attempted here, of what happened to the family after he brought his mother's crystal to England. This has been made so much clearer by this therapeutic photographic exploration that shows a very close, interdependent family. I can too easily, like my father, throw away that which is precious to me, as I thought I had done with his overcoat and appear to have done with the only photographs when I digitally transferred them into this book, and fear I have recently done with what l hope to end with.

I would like to hope that I have not unconsciously spread to my family (particularly my wife Jane and our now grown children, Lola, Lucy, and John-Louis and, through them, their children Sophie, Sam, and others to come), friends, colleagues, and acquaintances more detrimental trauma than helpfulness, but I know I have done both. Here's hoping through what I have now discovered to be more responsible to others and myself. But before I can sum up with the crystal, I realise there is something I must do which my father could not.

As I mentioned earlier, in my early twenties (and still now) I sought out relatives my father had stayed distant from, and on returning from meeting some I had found in North America, I told my father who had unnecessarily, but I think with love, met me at the airport when I returned home that they had told me they had seen his parents and sister's concentration camp death certificates. On reflection, it must have been horrific for my father to have been met, in wanting to meet me, with what I presented as a revelation I thought he had not known. I was therefore going to conclude with photographs of Eduard, Adele, and Hilde's death certificates from their concentration camps, which I found my father had all along. But I cannot, as I have now lost them. So instead, I conclude with the dates and places where this family – my family –was born and was killed or died, followed by a photograph of our crystal to signify this.

Eduard Loewenthal, born 10th February 1868, Braunbusch, Bohemia, Czech Republic. Killed 10 October 1942, Auschwitz, Poland.

Adele Loewenthal nee Loewy, 18 July 1882, Blstein/Eger, Bohemia, Czech Republic. Killed 19 October 1942, Auschwitz, Poland.

Hilde Loewenthal, born 7 December 1912, Bordenbach/Elbe, Bohemia, Czech Republic. Killed 26 October 1942, Treblinka, Poland.

Louis Loewenthal, born 3 September 1911, Bordenbach/Elbe, Bohemia, Czech Republic. Died 27 March 1986, Hammersmith, London, England.

Derek (Del) Loewenthal, born 3 October 1947, Hammersmith, London, England.

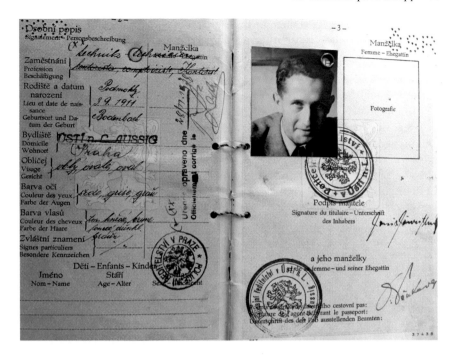

Photo 5.14 Passport photograph taken before the war

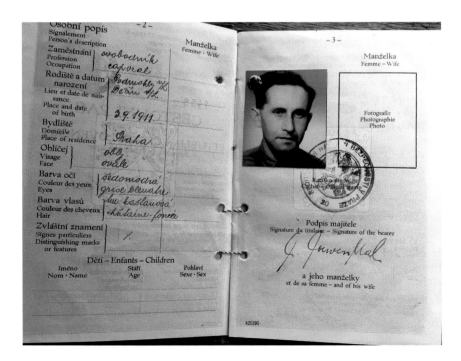

Photo 5.15 Passport photograph taken after the war

Conclusion (1): The Kristallnacht Carrier – resumé and what did I learn about myself - 'remembering, repeating and working through'?

Through carrying out the Kristallnacht carrier project, I am clearer as to why I find it difficult not to lose things of value for me – from a photograph to a cheque to, sometimes, a relationship. I have a Jewish surname, though it has been difficult for me to appropriately identify with it. The Jewish tradition is matrilineal, and whilst my father was Jewish, my mother was a Church of England London cockney, and from the ages four to fourteen, Welsh Chapel. This meant that, whilst Jews did not accept me as Jewish, everyone else assumed I was.

As described above, I was the first Loewenthal of my line, at least from the 1700s, not to be born in Bohemia. As mentioned in the previous story within a story my father was on holiday in France when Hitler invaded the Sudetenland. This was the time of Chamberlain's 'peace in our time', when Britain, and through us France, reneged on their agreement that an attack on one of them was an attack on all of them. As a result, Hitler invaded some of the German speaking areas of Czechoslovakia. Not only did the Czech soldiers not fight, despite being a significant fighting force, with Czechoslovakia at the time being one of the largest industrial powers in Europe, but having been completely surrounded by mountains, no longer had natural defences (perhaps, metaphorically, in some ways similar to what was to happen to my father and, to a lesser extent, myself). It was as if other countries had agreed for Hitler to occupy Kent, Surrey, and Sussex on the understanding that he promised not to cross the county boundaries.

Most significantly, Kristallnacht soon followed. As previously recounted, my father eventually escaped with great difficulty to London, wearing the coat (I still have) and the jacket (shown in the photograph of me as my father), and carrying with him an extraordinary amount of his mother's heavy Czech crystal, all of which I still have and examples of which are in the cover and other photographs. However, from the moment when my father learnt that his parents and sister had been murdered in the concentration camps in Poland he was a changed man. This perhaps can be gauged by contrasting the two passport photographs found after completing the above book (Photos 5.15 and 5.16): One taken before the war is of an energetic young man, full of the joys of life, managing to get away with a picture that really shouldn't have been accepted as a passport photograph. The second, taken after he heard the horrendous news, is of a broken man. From that day of returning to Prague, my father was no longer able to talk of his parents or sister to anyone. He also found it very difficult to have anything of value in his life that was important to him. I think now this was because of the fear of the pain of loss. He didn't want to own a house, or have the books he once cherished, or even the rest of his mother's china, which a friend had kept for him in Prague. My mother said he didn't want children, and I got a strong sense from him both of him not wanting me to pass exams but also his unbearable pain when I didn't do as well as I might have.

As a photographer and psychotherapist, phototherapy and therapeutic photography enable these interests to be combined. The Kristallnacht project of exploring re-enactment phototherapy encouraged me to dress as my father, grandfather, grandmother, and aunt based on a photograph of each that my father originally brought to England. Through this, I started to tell, in their voices, their stories as I imagined them from when my father left Czechoslovakia to the moment of their deaths. Already things were changing; I had never previously called them 'my grandfather, grandmother, and aunt' but rather 'my father's parents and sister'. Now, with trepidation, they were becoming 'Eduard, Adele, and Hilde'. Initially, it seemed important to me to be my father dressed as his parents and sister, each telling their stories. It wasn't easy to do, and it can still be raw when going, as now, back into it. I was very fortunate though in being trained as a psychotherapist and having a very supportive environment. I know Rosy Martin, a founder of re-enactment phototherapy, who wisely suggested I 'take it slowly' when I first described my intention for this project. I also have a very supportive wife and a community of psychotherapists who could hold and help me when required. There were many other vital influences through the wonderfully enriching suggestions of my tutors in the University of the Arts/London College of Communications MA programme in Documentary Photography and Photojournalism, who helped both visually and theoretically. I also became very influenced by W.G. Sebald's story, as well as the placing of his photos in his novel *Austerlitz*: Unlike the rest of this handbook, I managed (only just!) to place the Kristallnacht photos in this 'book within a book' without directly referring to them in the text. I also wish to acknowledge the influence of Marian Hirsch's post-memory regarding effects on children of the Holocaust as well as other photographic explorations and what we now call post-truth.

Questions of post-truth arose for me when, halfway through this project, I discovered a suitcase in the attic. In this, I found letters from my aunt, grandparents, and great-grandmother to my father when he was in England. I also found there the death certificates from the concentration camp, but, characteristically, I have now lost these, together with the four original photographs that my father had initially carried with him to England. The letters were in modern and in old German, and I was very fortunate in getting them translated by a fellow student and his mother. What emerged was a very close, loving family who would sometimes write several times a week. Just to gently touch and smell these letters and, in particular, see their signatures already brought my family into being. For example, my grandfather would sign off the letters to my father 'with deep kisses', and my grandmother would endlessly complain that my father, her son, didn't write enough. As their lives got worse, they appeared not to alarm my father, speaking just of the monotony and staying in bed in the day to keep warm. They also showed their resilience, as in this account in the above Kristallnacht book of my aunt Hilde, which has affected me the most and I repeat here:

> I'm convinced that maybe if we demand much maybe we reach at least something. I always come up with the story of the two flies who fall in the pot of milk. One killed herself in the instant but the second one started treading in her fight for survival and she got ground below her feet as an island of butter was created and she could reach the rescuing shore. I want to be the second fly and by speeding up I want to try to remain on the surface.

I found there were factual aspects that I had got wrong in imagining their story. For example, I thought my father had carried the typewriter I still have; but, in fact his family had sent it to him after he had arrived in England. I was also enabled to realise that my grandparents had been killed one week apart, but I had written of them being gassed holding each other. I did not change my accounts in the book, partly to document accurately how I had imagined them when I had dressed as them, but also because of the limits of my own emotional capacity. In writing the book *The Kristallnacht Carrier*, I did remove the unexpected number of times I initially I found I had told the story of one Sunday when I was about twelve years old, dressing up in black and standing in front of my father who was reading the newspaper and doing a Heil Hitler salute. I am reminded of Freud's (1914) 'Remembering, repeating and working-through'. There was always for me the intriguing question regarding my patients/clients and, here, myself when the 'repeating' is told in a way that is 'working through' and when it is told in a way that is a defence against doing just that. I still have not worked through all of this and hence my need for some repetition in this resumé. I have, though, been able to bring my relatives to life whilst hopefully being both truthful and ethically respectful, raising questions regarding Levinas' ethics (Loewenthal 2022) as putting the other first when it concerns those who are dead. (There have also been unexpected benefits: In the wake of Brexit, I am currently, albeit very reluctantly, applying for both German and Czech passports – something I could not have contemplated prior to this project). I don't know when I'll be able to put Eduard, Adele, and Hilde fully at rest, but bringing them alive through re-enactment phototherapy has certainly very much helped. I am, however, still conflicted in wanting to do this soon and yet knowing that premature closure would be worse. I would strongly recommend anyone embarking on such a journey to have the support of those who are likely to have had their own personal therapy. I am also very concerned that in a world that seems increasingly on the brink of further Munich-like agreements with the accompanying hatred and destructiveness, and of which antisemitism has been a barometer, that publicly speaking of my Jewish roots and being counted as such is liberating. However, there is the danger that, as in my case of *The Kristallnacht Carrier*, it could also be an unconscious desire to destroy what is important for me.

Conclusion (2): The Kristallnacht Carrier – what did I learn about re-enactment phototherapy theory?

Re-enactment phototherapy can be seen as partly a development of phototherapy (Chapter 2) and therapeutic photography (Chapter 3).

I regard as essential Martin's description that 'photographs produced in re-enactment phototherapy provide an unfiltered connection with the unconscious, since what takes place within the phototherapy session is rooted in unconscious processes' (Martin 2013, in Loewenthal 2013). I am interested in considering this, along with Benjamin's optical unconsciousness, which describes how photography 'engages and shapes perception and lived experience, forms of seeing and unseeing, sovereignty and agency, and time and space [and] can help us grasp the revolutionary optical dynamic that permeates the domains of history and politics' (Smith and Sliwinski 2017: 3).

Importantly, coupled with such individual repression are forms of socially driven repression. Pink and Mackley (2014) describe how photo re-enactment research (on which they base their re-enactment video research) is 'firmly rooted in assisting the participants to make visible their everyday practices that are socially relegated to invisible spaces and labour'.

As Hogan again writes, 'Often, re-enactment phototherapy is interested in challenging dominant stereotypes and creating new, more empowering narratives which are told in a pictorial sequence and are frequently publicly exhibited – indeed, this work is displayed as a proclamation' (Martin 2013). [It] straddles the line between social science, research, political activism and art: Martin refers to herself as an 'artist/researcher' (Hogan 2015). Consequently, there is the question of what is meant by 'artist/researcher' whether with particular reference to 'empirical research', 'theoretical research' and 'practice research'.

I agree therefore with Pink and Mackley (2014: 149) when they argue that such re-enactment practices 'offer new ways to respond to methodological challenges related to the ongoingness and unstoppable flow of everyday life, [enabling] research participants to give new levels of self-awareness about their lives and feelings'. In this sense, this is what I have personally attempted with *The Kristallnacht Carrier*.

Conclusion (3): The Kristallnacht Carrier – what did I learn about re-enactment phototherapy practice?

The appropriateness of photographers carrying out re-enactment phototherapy

One of the distinctions made between phototherapy and therapeutic photography, often seen in this handbook, is that the former requires a trained psychotherapist, whereas this need not be the case with the latter. I have come across an increasing trend of calling what was phototherapy 'therapeutic photography', so anything can then be done by someone with little or no therapeutic training. Also, the point is often conveniently missed that in therapeutic photography, the client and the photographer were initially one and the same and did not necessarily require external facilitation. This not requiring external facilitation might be true with re-enactment phototherapy when done on oneself, but even then is, from my experience with *The Kristallnacht Carrier*, very desirable. Furthermore, if one is facilitating re-enactment phototherapy for another, then usually it is strongly recommended that one be a trained therapist who has had personal therapy. However, when such a therapist/facilitator is required, then what should their training be (see also Chapter 12)? Whilst there are those without a formal therapeutic training who appear very able and appropriate in working therapeutically, in general I would strongly recommend that the facilitator be a psychotherapist who has had training which involves their own personal therapy, and that this therapy is relational (psychoanalytic/psychodynamic, humanistic/integrative or existential) and not behavioural, systemic, or EMDR, where the focus is not directly intersubjective. Otherwise, there is an increased danger that the facilitator will, not necessarily consciously, inappropriately interfere with the path of the client through their own reactions and unexplored minefields. Furthermore, I was aware in carrying out this project that

I am in an environment surrounded by therapeutic support systems, where I was and am able to be held and speak of thoughts and feelings that may not be acceptable in ordinary conversation.

The conflict between personal versus professional deadlines

I was very fortunate in being able to speak to Rosie Martin at the beginning of this project and her words helpfully stayed with me – 'take it slowly'. When working something through therapeutically, there is very often an iterative process involving insight and then, sometimes, a closing up/resistance. I often, for example, found myself, initially unknowingly, repeating myself in the Kristallnacht book and in particular family stories. I understand this as my starting to explore an emotional concern and repeating this in a way showed that I was sometimes getting stuck, as I was unable to be clear. I think this is common in psychotherapy, and I have also witnessed this in phototherapy groups where the client emotionally repeats what they are triggered by, for example by showing the same family photograph but being unable to continue to work it through. Whilst progress can depend on the abilities of the facilitator, it is also very individual. What can take one person minutes can take another years to work through. Hence, external deadlines are often not helpful here. When completing such emotional processes through photography, an external deadline such as a publication, customer requirement, or due date of an academic assignment can be inappropriate and potentially emotionally damaging.

There were times when I did not wish to think about the project but felt pressured by the approaching deadlines. However, it was not always clear when this was the reason or when such deadlines were also helpful in preventing my unconscious attempts at premature closure.

Potential conflict in terms of 'who is the project for?'

Again, following from the last point, re-enactment phototherapy must be for the client, rather than any other audience. Yet other audiences can be there and interfere with the process. Thus, for example, as mentioned previously, I found to my surprise that several times I repeated the same story, not as a literary device but because I appeared to forget. Whilst this was therapeutically useful, it would have not been conducive to the reader if left unaltered. My experience is that it is best if one first writes and photographs for oneself and one's own emotional processes, then, and only when some emotional steady state is reached, should it be modified for other audiences.

This two-stage process also happened in taking the actual re-enactment photographs. The first time I dressed as my father, grandparents, and aunt, I just photographed with an iPad and was very emotional in starting this journey (see Chapter 9). Subsequently, I retook these photographs in a studio, partly to show others. On the second shoot, whilst my emotional experiences were very different, they were still very therapeutically helpful. However, the 'professional' temptation is to only show the studio photos, which could then be considered as more 'post-truth'.

Conclusion (4): The Kristallnacht Carrier – post-script

Just before submitting the manuscript for this book, I went to the cemetery where my father is buried after a long absence due to COVID. I then wrote the following to our grown-up children:

> On going to the cemetery last Thursday, I realise how much my feelings towards my father have changed, I think in large part due to the Kristallnacht photo project. I feel just love, warmth and gratitude to him now – no knots and some compensatory thoughts previously seem just wrong!
>
> . . . I would like please to be buried in the same cemetery – but hopefully not for a while!

References

Dennett, T. (2013). Chapter 3, Jo Spence's camera therapy: Personal therapeutic photography as a response to adversity. In D. Loewenthal (ed.), *Phototherapy and Therapeutic Photography in a Digital Age*, pp. 31–39. Hove: Routledge.

Freud, S. (1914). Remembering, repeating and working-through. *Standard Edition*, 6: 147–156.

Heron, J. (1980). History & development of co-counselling. *Self & Society*, 8(4): 99–106.

Hirsch, M. (2012). *The Generation of Postmemory: Writing and Visual Culture After the Holocaust.* New York: Columbia University Press.

Hogan, S. (2015). *Art Therapies a Critical Introduction.* Abingdon: Routledge.

Hogan, S. (2022). *Photography.* Bingley: Emerald Publishing.

Loewenthal, D. (ed.). (2013). *Phototherapy and Therapeutic Photography in a Digital Age.* Hove: Routledge.

Loewenthal, D. (2022). *Levinas and the Other in Psychotherapy and Counselling.* Abingdon: Routledge.

Martin, R. (2013). Inhabiting the image: Photography, therapy and re-enactment photography. In D. Loewenthal (ed.), *Phototherapy and Therapeutic Photography in a Digital Age*, pp. 69–81. Hove: Routledge.

Martin, R., and Spence, J. (1987). *Double Exposure: The Minefield of Memory.* London: Photographer's Gallery (Exhibition and Catalogue).

Martin, R., and Spence, J. (1988). Phototherapy as a healing art. In L. Wells (ed.), *The Photography Reader.* London and New York: Routledge.

Moreno, J. (1946 [2020]). *Psychodrama*, volume 1. Princeton: Psychodrama Press.

Moustakas, C. (1990). *Heuristic Research: Design, Methodology and Application.* Newbury Park, CA: Sage.

The One Project. (2020). *Therapeutic Photography.* https://theoneproject.co/therapeutic-photography/. Accessed 2 September 2022.

Perls, F., Hefferline, R., and Goodman, P. (1973). *Gestalt Therapy: Excitement and Growth in the Human Personality.* London: Pelican.

Pink, S., and Mackley, K. (2014). Re-enactment methodologies for everyday life research: Art therapy insights for video ethnography. *Visual Studies*, 29(2): 146–154.

Sebald, W. G. (2018 [2001]). *Austerlitz*. London: Penguin.

Sherlock, A. (2012). Jo Spence. *Frieze Magazine*, Issue 149, September. www.frieze.com/issue/review/jo-spence/.

Smith, S., and Sliwinski, S. (eds.). (2017). *Photography and the Optical Unconscious*. London: Duke University Press.

Spence, J. (1986). *Putting Myself in the Picture: A Political, Personal and Photographic Autobiography*. London: Camden Press.

Winckler, J. (2013). Chapter 11, 'the time we were not born': Experimental archaeology – working within and beyond the photographic archive with photography students. In D. Loewenthal (ed.), *Phototherapy and Therapeutic Photography in a Digital Age*, pp. 128–142. Hove: Routledge.

Winckler, J., and Conway, S. (2006). Acts of embodiment. In D. Barndt (ed.), *Wild Fire: Art as Activism*, pp. 205–220. Toronto: Sumach Press. ISBN 1894549554. https://theoneproject.co.

6 Therapeutic photo diaries/ photo journaling

Summary

This chapter demonstrates the use of a photo diary through the author's exploration of the personal, the political, and the professional as a result of the COVID lockdown. This is followed by some information as to the potential benefits of photo diaries and how to go about creating them.

Once again, what is important is what emerges between the person and the photograph. This unique phenomenology from often pre-conscious associations can give rise to descriptions that couldn't be otherwise derived. Though once voiced, it is usually clear they were there all along!

Key learning points

1. Photo diaries represent an approach whereby photos provide a catalyst for eliciting thoughts and feelings that might otherwise not emerge.
2. Photo diaries can uniquely evoke accompanying accounts of experiences varying from the use of a service to a holiday.
3. What is important is what an individual makes of the photograph. It is their perception that is important and, like with other therapeutic uses of photographs, there is no universal reading. The same photograph can have very different meanings for different people.

Exercise

Take a photo of yourself when you wake up and a photo before you go to sleep. For each photo, write about what you see. Repeat for seven days.

COVID case study: The personal, the political, and the professional – a photo diary exploration

At the start of COVID, when the travel curfew came into force, my wife and I were separated through working in different locations. This was by far the longest amount of time – over 14 weeks – for us not to be together in over 40 years. During this enforced separation, I kept a photo diary by taking a daily photograph with my phone.

DOI: 10.4324/9781003240914-7

The first photo I took (during my then newly initiated habit of jogging) was of two shorn-off trees (Photo 6.1). So much had been and was to be shorn off.

I had not, and have not, recovered from BREXIT shearing off our cultural and economic future with Europe (and the world). In an attempt to mitigate this, I had successfully, and reluctantly, applied for dual British and now Czech nationality. But, because of COVID restrictions, the planned initial trip to the Czechia with our son couldn't happen. Now, it looks as if our Czech future will remain shorn off and, as with those trees, will at best be experienced as stunted growth.

My jogging was mainly around a local park's blind garden, where I was to get on nodding terms, together with the occasional brief pleasantry, with a growing group (until the police broke them up) who may have come from some form of sheltered accommodation. Later, on one of my jogging days, there appeared in that garden the graffiti: 'WE ARE PLAGUE', (Photo 6.1) which might be taken as an expression of wretched isolation, and on another day was painted 'NO LOVE' (Photo 6.1).

Subsequently, when I was allowed to reconnect with my family and as with others allowed to meet in small groups, I still went for my park jogs. But now I wondered what it must be like for those who still did not have anyone, to see what otherwise might be viewed as picturesque, happy, reunited groups sitting in varying circles on the grass in the sun with their friends. It was too much for me to contemplate taking that photo!

One of the most difficult decisions was to voluntarily be shorn of our grandchildren and not help our daughter with them. But what is it like for children who were learning to ask who and what they could touch and couldn't have other children at their birthday parties (Photo 6.1)? And ZOOM birthday celebrations as in Photo 6.1 – weren't birthday celebrations!

I was also in those early days of COVID isolation struck by and took my daily phone photo sometimes of flowers in the house (again projecting onto them). In

Photo 6.1a Two shorn off trees   *Photo 6.1b* 'WE ARE PLAGUE'

Photo 6.1c 'NO LOVE'   *Photo 6.1d* Zoom birthday celebrations

Photo 6.1e Birthday party

Photo 6.1 (Continued)

becoming separated from my wife, the daffodils went from appearing vibrantly male and female (Photo 6.2) to dead and withered (Photo 6.2), and, occasionally, feelings of not wanting another day like this arose (Photo 6.2). However, there were also many days of great joy and inspiration and seeing the beautiful (Photo 6.2). Yet sometimes, this beauty could also be twinged with sadness (Photo 6.2). I then found myself being called to look at a poinsettia (Photo 6.2) which had more than survived two Christmas's (as I was similarly resolving to do!). Eventually, house plants and herbs, whilst beautiful, seemed to now be reminding me to keep my distance (Photo 6.2).

Regarding my professional work, there were downsides to not meeting in the flesh, at least for the client to not have somewhere to go, yet to my surprise, through

Photo 6.2a Vibrantly male and   *Photo 6.2b* Dead and withered   *Photo 6.2c* Not wanting another
             female   day like this

Photo 6.2d Seeing the beautiful   *Photo 6.2e* Twinged with sadness   *Photo 6.2f* Poinsettia

 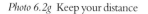

Photo 6.2g Keep your distance   *Photo 6.2h* Fascistic, misogynistic, egotist?

COVID, my professional work flourished. I chair a critical existential-analytic psychotherapy training programme (safpac.co.uk), and we went online and it worked (and there was more work!). We've just had a conference which, thanks to ZOOM, became a truly international conference. Further, COVID frontline workers accessed therapy for the first time through a free service we set up. Also, I (somewhat crazily) published more than ever.

However, perhaps most importantly, my online psychotherapy practice, despite the important lack of aura which is only possible with physical presence, has changed and mainly for the better. There is more equality in my practice now. Whereas previously, the client was sitting or lying on the couch a COVID distance away, now we are an equal distance, closer and more equal. I've also had reinforced that working with transference and the like is still possible, whilst being less 'blank screen', though perhaps more difficult at first to hear.

Returning to my personal life, when my wife and I were allowed to get back together, it wasn't easy, as we had both been even more used to doing things our own way, but we came to love each other again, replenished for the better by our COVID experiences. Yet, our children and grandchildren had learnt to live without us, and whilst in our family our love for each other had, I would like to think, too solid a basis to be fundamentally threatened, there was now a new accelerated independence. This may be good for them, but as through BREXIT my country has altered its relations with the world, through COVID, our family relations may have become prematurely diminished.

Yet, my family and I are so much luckier than most, as through COVID there is increasingly disrupted personal development, loneliness, economic suffering, and even far more famine and death to come worldwide. Moreover, there is an increasingly dominant political reaction which, rather than focussing on collectively working for the common good to combat COVID, nuclear war, climate change, etc. instead, is promoting populism and individualism. This ideology is becoming so insidiously 'the new normal' that even the teddy bears that we put in our windows because of COVID for the children walking by to see appear increasingly able to transform into fascistic, misogynistic, egotists (Photo 6.2). So, is this a moment when, through COVID, I and others are, apparently, against our wishes, having a better glimpse of the reality of our human brokenness that was already there? Hope not!!!

Conclusion

I would again like to conclude with some useful information from two of the growing number of related websites and publications that may be of interest to those involved in phototherapy and therapeutic photography in general, as well as specifically here regarding photo diaries and photo journaling.

Anita Chaudhuri (2022) points to three areas of research which are of interest to phototherapy and therapeutic photography in general as well as specifically here regarding photo diaries/photo journaling.

First '. . . research from Lancaster University reveals that taking a photo every day and sharing it online increases wellbeing. Participants reported greater self-care,

community interaction and enjoyment of opportunities to reminisce' (Brewster and Cox 2019).

Secondly '. . . a study at Yale University found that when people take photos of experiences, they enjoy them more and are more engaged with the activity' (Diehl et al. 2016).

Thirdly,

By its very nature, the practice grounds you in the present. Research from Harvard Business School shows that when contemplating objects in the moment, we think visually whereas, when our mind drifts to the future, the brain moves into the realm of language.

(Amit et al. 2017)

Here are what I consider some usual pointers from Ronna Jevne (2020):
"Every image has an echo. Every echo has an image.

Options for photo-journaling
1. Photo Essays
   Select a theme or a question. Gather or shoot photos that for some reason relate to the theme. You can write about each image in the collection or wait until the images have a collective voice.
2. Poems
   Create an alphabet poem evoked by the photograph. Or reverse the process. Write a poem. Then capture an image of the tone and message of the poem.
3. Give yourself an assignment
   A wound not healed/A hope fulfilled/A story that needs telling/My favourite things/What I cannot say /A prayer for peace/Life through the eyes of a three-year-old
4. Tell a story
   Do a "random shoot". Photograph for a day or more whatever catches your eye. Then ask yourself to tell a story with the images. Arrange them in the order that reveals itself and tell the story that the images are making visible.
5. Create a dialogue
   Select two parts of the photo. They could be two people but they could be between two objects in the photo. For example, between a horse and the fence; between a dark cloud and a setting sun. Create a dialogue between them.
6. Create a cluster
   Place a photography in the centre of your page. Create multiple spokes around that help you understand the associations that come to mind as you look at the image. Write about one or more of the words or phrases that come to mind.
The options are endless."

References

Amit, E., Hoeflin, C., Hamzah, N., and Fedorenko, E. (2017). An asymmetrical relationship between verbal and visual thinking: Converging evidence from behavior and fMRI. *NeuroImage*, 152: 619–627.

Brewster, L., and Cox, A. M. (2019). The daily digital practice as a form of self-care: Using photography for everyday well-being. *Health (London, England: 1997)*, 23(6): 621–638.

Chaudhuri, A. (2022). Photo journaling for mental health: Benefits, ideas and tips. *Psychologies*, 15 March. www.psychologies.co.uk/photo-journaling-for-mental-health/.

Diehl, K., Zauberman, G., and Barasch, A. (2016). *How Taking Photos Increases Enjoyment of Experiences*. www.createwritenow.com/journal-writing-blog/how-to-journal-your-way-to-achieving-any-goal-0-0.

Jevne, R. (2020). *Photo-Journaling: Images and Echoes*. Creative Now, 8 October. www.createwritenow.com/journal-writing-blog/how-to-journal-your-way-to-achieving-any-goal-0-0.

7 Professional and personal development

The use of photography in coaching, training, and team and management development

Summary

This chapter is about facilitating personal and professional development through photography. It primarily focuses on the author's work with an international company who commissioned expensive processing plants throughout the world. The problem, which an application of Photocards was designed to solve, involved project managers who were normally engineers needing to have more of the language of the various stakeholders to further ensure that the upfront design met their needs. There was a danger that if the plant was mainly designed from an engineering perspective, subsequent changes once commissioning had started could easily lead to significantly increased costs in the reconstruction. Photocards were used in one-to-one meetings with project managers (on this occasion, I used www.spectrovisio.net/eng/#cards) to enable them to develop their language and be able to communicate with stakeholders from the initiation of the planning process. Further examples are briefly given of the use of Photocards to enable groups to explore difficult topics and uses in discussion groups, training, and team development.

Key learning points

1. Photocards can be useful to enable elicitation in numerous contexts, including discussion groups, team development, and research.
2. Photocards can be used to elicit evaluations: For example, 'Choose a Photocard from the set that best describes how you feel about this course/situation/person/controversial topic etc.'
3. Photocards can be used to plan future actions: For example, 'Choose a Photocard that best describes how you see either your situation or team or your current skills. Now, choose a Photocard that best represents how you would like to see your situation or team or your skills'.
4. Photocards can enable communication individually and particularly in groups, helping users to both find words and share them, which otherwise would not happen.
5. As with therapeutic clients, it is not uncommon for coaching work clients to have trauma of a previous work experience going wrong which is difficult for

DOI: 10.4324/9781003240914-8

them to work through and, on occasion, interferes with their ability to accept they may have made a mistake.

6. Photocards can facilitate work clients having space to talk about their anxieties with others at work and, sometimes, address what these people may think of them.

7. Photocards can facilitate managers and other work clients having a space to talk about related aspects of their personal life, though, in a coaching context, it is considered best to have a work task as apparently a central focus to return to.

8. There is a key issue regarding agendas in that it is assumed to be good practice for the phototherapist not to have an agenda for the client. However, there is a danger of the coach et al. being degenerate in that they may attempt to appear to not have an agenda for the client whilst being influenced by how they will be measured by the organisation or different person who is paying for their services.

9. I could not have done this work if I had not spent many years of my life as a management consultant/coach – the photographs are often a great aid to this, but as with psychotherapy, they are an aid and not a practice in their own right.

Exercise

Consider a specific situation which in some way is problematic for you. Choose a Photocard (from for example: one of the 52 Talking Pictures located at www.dello ewenthal.com/phototherapy-and-therapeutic-photography.html) of how you are feeling in general or about this situation and write down how come this Photocard called to you and your associated thoughts. Now choose another Photocard of how you wished you were feeling and again write down how come this Photocard called to you and your associated thoughts.

The use of photography in coaching

Over many years I have at times been using Photocards in coaching/management and team development. It was therefore reaffirming to read research carried out by Donaldson-Wright and Hefferon (2020) claiming 'that using photographs in coaching enriched the coaching experience, extending engagement and participation; cultivated mindful self-awareness and enhanced positivity' (Donaldson-Wright and Hefferon 2020: 166). As they so helpfully conclude:

> Photographs have a number of unique qualities that make them a potentially powerful tool for use in coaching. . . . Some or all of these qualities are known and have been applied by other professionals working in psychotherapy, social work and qualitative research. . . . For example, innovative applications of photography are used in counsellor education, 'to enhance the development of self, professional identity and multicultural awareness in trainee counsellors' (Schmidt et al. 2019: 105) and within medical education, 'to enhance reflective practice and professional development with GP [General Practitioner] trainees

(Rutherford et al. 2018: 158). This serves as recognition of the growing potential of using photography in professional settings.

(Donaldson-Wright and Hefferon 2020: 179)

The case study

Central to my research in a multinational company was my work with six project managers who were offered one two-hour session followed by five weekly one-hour sessions (This format of a two-hour first meeting and then weekly, monthly, or termly follow-up meetings is what I have found previously useful in my experience of coaching mainly chief executives and medical consultants). Much of the work was face-to-face, with the option of it being at the head office or my location, whereas others overseas were on Skype or telephone and sometimes face-to-face when they came back to the UK.

This assignment was exploring the use of photographs to help senior project managers further develop their abilities to successfully manage the front-end of building multi-million-pound manufacturing plants in different locations throughout the world. These project managers are usually from an engineering background, which hadn't always prepared them for allowing enough time to check with all the stakeholders up front regarding the various designs of what was to be implemented. In common with most projects, the more time spent reaching an agreement of what was to be done at the start, the greater the chance that what was built would optimally meet the various stakeholders' requirements. However, there was too often the concern that if project manager engineers thought they knew what was right, it was difficult for them to go and check this against what a stakeholder wanted; all the more so if the engineer thought the stakeholder would have different ideas!

What follows are my notes taken afterwards (those for meeting five are missing!) with one of the project managers with identifying details modified. (All those I coached, as well as their employing organisation, gave permission for my work with them to be published.)

I hope these sometimes rambling notes may give some idea of how this is a different kind of work from what has been presented previously, which has focussed on the individual as a client, and give a feel of the work and some of its vital 'nooks and crannies'.

Linda: Meeting 1

This first two-hour session was conducted on the telephone, as Linda said there was not a good enough signal for Skype. I had therefore previously sent her a selection of photographs by email.

At the start, Linda sounded a little bored and unmotivated; however, she turned out to be a good example of someone who didn't find it easy to speak about what she might want to learn, and when she chose the photograph of the bag of onions (Photo 7.1a), this brought a facilitative new dimension. As will be shown, she was able to play with this photograph, seeing herself being constrained by the bag but also eventually able to see how she might be constraining others. She was then able to give good examples, through a photograph of the blue sky (Photo 7.1b) and others of a path amongst some trees (Photo 7.1d) and of a railway line (Photo 7.1c), as to where she would like to be. Linda started by giving a very professional-appearing key list of learning needs, stating she needed to have:

'1. A better understanding of stakeholders' needs
2. Better communication with the stakeholder
3. Able to follow through on actions'.

She then added: 'There was a problem because the key stakeholder was worried about cost but others above me are worried about the schedule. Usually with costing there is an allowance for contingencies, but the stakeholder wants the cheapest options and questions why have so much contingency'.

Linda continued, 'It's the role of the project manager to ensure sub cost contingency for design variability is there from the start. My department wants enough money at the start without having to go back for more – the first figure you give tends to stick. When the resource director/regional manager hands over this is not a clear moment. The resource director sees you as starting to end your current job as you start the new one – but in practice it is a grey area with a hand over. Or at least it can feel like that'.

On this project, I had another consideration: Did I want to take it? It is a big upheaval – I had been handling a project which had been around, so changing was stressful. Though, on the other hand, previously in the UK I had lived a long way from HQ, and there is only so much you can do on the phone from home.

There are nine stages of the project route map – step three is the concept stage regarding the front end – once you've got a final concept, the front end finishes – you shouldn't go for project funding until the end of stage four. However, because of political pressure, you had to get it all ready. It took a while to educate the stakeholder. If we are going to go early, it is difficult to persuade the sponsor that one needs extra contingency. It took education on both sides because the regional director came out to the USA. It carried a lot of weight.

The downfall at the earliest stages is when you tell the stakeholder what you want to hear. What is important is getting through the concept stage. Concept costs always gave plus or minus ten percent. It is important for me to keep communicating with the stakeholder – education of the stakeholder so

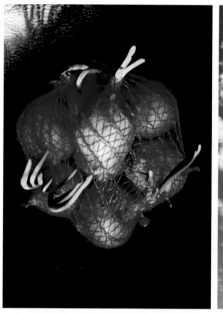

Photo 7.1a Bag of onions

Photo 7.1b Blue sky

Photo 7.1c Railway line

Photo 7.1d The path amongst some trees

he is aware of what can be in or out given the budget arrived at. He had a big surprise: He had £11M in mind and we said £15M! The stakeholder reports to a vice president . . . important in terms of my own development.

Del: 'Could you choose a photograph that calls to you with regard to an area of competence you would like to develop?'

Linda chose from the attachment I had sent her. 'This picture (Photo 7.1a) – it could be that I have been in the company 15 years – who knows – those onions have been in that position for a long time.

Linda: 'In terms of projects, I remember a previous project which was liberating. We weren't constrained by the management of negotiations – it was very successful, whereas this project and the previous project you are very much constrained – this person signs this off etc. rather than you have the freedom to develop it. If you don't mange carefully you spend all your time justifying your project. Sometimes you feel there is so many people internally you have got to be careful not to spend all your time justifying. There are rules and regulations. For example, there is a set of quality guidelines, so you need to get technical people involved in the front end. The project manager says it is about growing the new shoots in our industry. It reminds me I've got some garlic bulbs in the fridge I must plant out'.

Del: 'Which photograph comes to mind in terms of where you would like to be in terms of your competence with regard to the front end of projects?'

Linda: 'I assume it would be the photograph of the blue sky (Photo 7.1b) . . . [pause] the expanse where you have got more freedom [pause] but it's not going to happen in the realm of project management. Maybe then the photograph of the forest (Photo 7.1d). The path through the forest – there are trees there, but you have the freedom to pass through without getting stuck in the trees. Blue sky thinking is by definition what you are aiming for. I guess the path is when you can see a clear route from the beginning of the path to the end of it – but there is still a path there. It needs to be like the railway line (Photo 7.1c)'. [A very popular choice of project managers!].

Del: 'What are the forces against seeing and staying with the path?'

Linda didn't answer directly at first:

Linda: 'Understanding all the variables that need to be included in the project for example the wall being painted white [pause] I try very hard not to . . . when someone senior has reported something not to jump around'. (Linda then went into reinforcing how she was a good manager.)

Del: 'What about strengths in yourself?'

Linda: 'Experience – learning from previous projects – getting the job done – reliability. I'm not a 9 to 5 person in project delivery. If there is a confrontation, I want to get to it there and then, but if it is a big decision I like to wait till the next day, also just picking up the phone and talking to people – not just a cold email.

'The concept stage will be finished in the next few weeks, the scheme design completed in late June. You get more senior people off your back when costs are agreed and now it is more pleasurable you then get the freedom to design facilities'.

Del: ' "Freedom" is a word that seems important for you Linda. Is it that if you feel constrained all the time it is not much of a career?'

Linda: 'I am the owner of the bag and know when to put it round the onions, but it is important for me to listen to peoples' opinions – there again if people want gold plating, they can't have it'.

Linda: Meeting 2

Linda started by saying that she had settled in better in the new job and that she had found useful the photograph of the bag of onions with the green shoots and the path across the forest. I also asked if she had planted the garlic bulbs that she had told me about that were in her fridge. Linda replied 'yes'. I then said, 'I suppose it's more about planting those garlic bulbs that are you?' But seeing this was perhaps getting too personal, I quickly changed to,

> 'What would you like to explore? There is an hour. It can be talking through a particular task or developing a skill. As you know, your organisation doesn't have a particular action plan for you to carry out. They are interested in improving front-end delivery, but it can be anything that you think can help you as a project manager'.

Linda said she had a difficult meeting the next day as she had to tell a long-standing contractor that they hadn't got the job. This contractor did have other work on site, and there was a question of how, as I more than reflected back, 'they might opt out now if they didn't get the big new contract'.

I asked if there were any other contracts in the pipeline, but it turned out there was only a smaller one. Linda said that she would have to speak to this contractor on the phone, whereas she prefers face-to-face. I suggested different ways of responding to the contractor and how this contractor would have to break the news to his own organisation. We also discussed budgets and I asked some questions about them. Linda also looked at how another contractor might be good as the policeman for the new project. Linda said she found all this useful. (I found myself offering potential ways of solving problems – very different from counselling! I also found myself using such management language as 'critical path', 'budgeting', etc.)

Linda: Meeting 3

Linda explored her concern regarding whether to escalate an issue to senior management regarding a particular processing machine from another country. She felt she had, to date, presented this to people 'who couldn't hear, but it's knowing when to press the button as an escalation'. [Where to escalate is important for front-end success but can make the project manager appear they can't cope]. Instead of continuing exploring whether to escalate, Linda switched topics and went back to another aspect of the project she had mentioned in a previous session. Linda said she needed to get someone in as a contractor to help with design. They now realised that the second line they had to put in would affect the first line, but they didn't want a delay on putting in the first line. The current project was budgeted at £16 million, now potentially £32 million, and there was also another project down the road.

Linda: Meeting 4

Linda wanted to talk again about escalation and senior managers trying to be helpful.

'When escalating, you tell the senior managers of a problem. But then you have to come up with reasons why the solutions are not working in practice'. I said, 'You can lose control'. Linda replied, 'You can then be subject to Chinese whispers around the HQ coffee machines'.

We then spoke of the supplier who had told Linda that there would be a four-week delay and now wanted a considerable larger payment, but Linda, thoughtfully and somewhat resignedly, added 'This supplier is the only one in the world with these machines'.

Linda, again using me as a sounding board, concluded,

'I can only get this machine now and help my organisation not get into this situation in the future. I also first need to both check that we do need it when I'm being told we do and offer this supplier a carrot of my organisation wanting these machines in the future. We will send someone over for six months to learn the process – so I'm writing a job spec for this. In future, I have to also consider the risks of demolition in terms of safety and manage all the key risks on the timeline'.

Overall, this session might be seen as Linda indirectly working through her experience of what had unfairly happened to her when she had previously escalated an issue, and being able to acknowledge to me, and hence to herself, that she couldn't always be in control and how best to respond to this.

Linda: Meeting 6

This was our last session, and we had agreed to review our work together.

Del: 'What do you want to develop further regarding your front-end skills?'
Linda: 'People management – I find talking to people – different traditions in workplaces – are difficult to talk about. Talking through with you has helped me to build my confidence and I have done the right thing. Peer reviews, having a third party, has been helpful.

'With regard to soft skills – talking it through helped me recognise the sizeable culture of difference between the USA and the UK. For example, we previously always used the same local contractor. But here, we have now gone to another consultant. On this site, they were prepared to do a different thing.

'We only used the photos in the first session – the not holding down progress and the green shoots (Photo: 7.1a). I was wondering whether my company was holding me back. You mentioned I said 'freedom' a lot; I hadn't realised this and it is important for me. So, although the net around the onions holds me back in terms of regulation, my company does give me more freedom. I also realise that I can be that net wrongly holding other people, and their potential green shoots, back.

'What we discussed about escalating the issue and losing control was important. I had previously once lost control of how it was seen in the UK, but this time I looked at it and it was the right thing to do.

'Show importance of front-end and judgement call on when to show your hand on escalation, but make sure you've done everything possible beforehand – but don't leave it until too late. You can't control what happens over the coffee machines at head office!

'Overall, I found it helpful. It was good to talk; the more I talked, I thought of things differently – I found it very helpful. What the photos demonstrate is that you inquire of your looking. The obvious one is the blue sky (Photo: 7.1b); it offers a different perspective, but talking to somebody hadn't previously been available. Also the railway line (Photo: 7.1c) and the path through the forest (Photo: 7.1d) – more the railway line – it's been refreshing to talk through some of the issues without being told what the rules of my organisation should be. You adapted the sessions to allow me to talk about what I wanted – it was good. I opened up to you more than to other people in my company – it was a different conversation'.

Conclusion: Some further thoughts on facilitating personal together with professional development

The aforementioned case study is just one example of facilitating personal and professional development through photography. Each project manager taking part in this management development programme was so different, and it was difficult to know who to choose for this chapter. Importantly, I was able to be in a situation with this international company not to have to have any covert company agendas for the consultees – I was able to be clear with everyone as to the organisation's reasons for inviting me to assist in this way with management development.

It does though seem potentially vital, as with therapy, to reinvent coaching with every client, every time. Nevertheless, what follows are some thoughts on coaching and associated practices using photographs with the hope they might sometimes have implications for others.

Unlike coaching, using photographs as part of counselling and psychotherapy can be a useful way of starting sessions in that they can reduce anxiety whilst channelling it to the projection on the photographs. In coaching/consulting, I find it far more often appropriate to first build a relationship and introduce the photographs more towards the end of the first session as a way of symbolising what is being said and providing a possible shorthand reference for future sessions. Also, in comparison to therapy, I found myself more likely to both suggest solutions and share my own experience. This enables me to provide some more therapeutic interventions, which, perhaps because of the more chatty style, appear more accepted and taken in.

A danger can be that the consultee, by divulging what they would not usually speak of, particularly within the politics of working contexts, is that I will become associated with this. The danger for me is that the consultee will defensively, often initially unconsciously, move to drop or discredit me. This also raises the more important question as to how voluntary the subject of such coaching/counselling/research interviews are. To what extent do people volunteer to please their bosses, and how confident should the client be of confidentiality? Sometimes, my own self-doubt is such that I wonder with some consultees about the possibility that the less confidential (though important to the consultee) information the consultee shares with me, the higher they will rate me!

Often managers, as with therapeutic clients, seem to have trauma from a previous experience of a project going wrong, which can be difficult but rewarding for them to work through (as with Linda earlier), and sometimes they struggle to accept they may have made a mistake.

It seems so important that consultees can have space to talk about their anxieties with other people, including sometimes addressing what these people may think of them. However, confidentiality is vital, and the coach et al. can be tempted and to say something about the consultee to another who could be influential regarding future contracts for the coach et al.

Often it was important for people to have a space to also talk about related aspects of their personal life, though when this was done, it was often through both of us keeping the work task as the central topic.

I am always amazed how photographs enable politically and personally sensitive thoughts to be communicated in acceptable ways. This occurs, in my experience, when, for example, working with teams whereby each member or sub-team chooses a Photocard of how they currently experience the team, and then, after sharing this with the team, chooses a Photocard of how they would like the team to be.

Perhaps one of the greatest uses of Photocards is that of formulating and communicating in discussion groups: What comes to mind through choosing photographs that group members then each share on a potentially divisive topic.

I could not have done this work if I had not spent many years of my life as a management consultant/facilitator – the photographs were often a great aid to this, but as with psychotherapy, they were an aid and not, for me, a practice in its own right.

I would like to think that this work using photographs leads to both personal and professional development. Overall, my experience is that adding the use of photographs to such professional practices as coaching, as well as psychotherapy etc., has made a very important contribution to the development of the majority of my consultees.

References

www.delloewenthal.com/phototherapy-and-therapeutic-photography.html.

Donaldson-Wright, M., and Hefferon, K. (2020). 'A new vision!': Exploring coachee experiences of using photography in coaching – an interpretative phenomenological analysis. *International Journal of Evidence Based Coaching and Mentoring*, 18(2).

Rutherford, Forde, E., Priego Hernandez, J., Butcher, A., and Wedderburn, C. (2018). Using photography to enhance GP trainees' reflective practice and professional development. *Medical Humanities*, 44: 158–164.

Schmidt, M. K., Murdock Bishop, J. L., and Becker, K. (2019). Using photography to enhance development of self, professional identity, and multicultural awareness. *Journal of Creativity in Mental Health*, 14(1): 105–114.

www.spectrovisio.net/eng/#cards.

8 The development of action plans through photography

Summary

Here, a case is given of the author working with a group of ex-inmates who have been given a psychiatric diagnosis and have joined a photographic group in order to find employment. Over two weekends, the group was briefly introduced to taking photographs with point and shoot cameras (see Figure 8.1). This was followed by an exploration of external forces, and then internal forces, that they perceived as helping and hindering them in getting employment. As part of this process, participants took photographs in order to help them clarify these internal and external forces. Then, through the use of force field analysis, they could prioritise which actions would be most productive in helping them get a job and which forces were acting against the chances of them getting work and needed to be addressed. A case study of one of the participants is provided. Photographs can similarly be used to develop community action.

Assignment

Write a short sentence describing an action you want to take. Now start thinking and making preliminary lists of what factors/forces are helping and what factors/forces are working against you in achieving this goal. Next, start to take photographs of these forces for and against you, and in doing so, finalise your lists of both (you can add some, subtract others, and firm up on those you weren't sure about). Then, draw a line to represent what you want to achieve. On one side, equally spaced out, name the forces for your goal, and on the other side of the line, the forces against it. Now, for each of the lists of forces, draw lines at right angles to your original line, each line's length equivalent to your guesstimate of the strength of that force. Next, look at 'the forces against': Which forces' lines, given your time and energy, can you most easily shorten (explore these, preferably with someone therapeutically informed)? And regarding 'the forces for': Which forces' lines, given your time and energy, can you most easily lengthen (again explore these, preferably with someone therapeutically informed)? Once you've done this, your goal is more likely to be reached!

DOI: 10.4324/9781003240914-9

Key learning points

1. As with most phototherapy and therapeutic photography, it's what the person makes of the photograph (and the creative making process) that is important rather than what is regarded as aesthetic.
2. It is again the interplay between images and written thoughts that leads the client/activist client to a new place
3. Such action plans can be created by an individual or a group/community, both for their own development and to influence others.

The development of action plans through photography: The case of photo-assisted employability/rehabilitation

The approach of using photographs to enhance emotional learning involves the client having a specific aim. In these cases, it was to get a job. The approach developed here was again influenced by PhotoVoice's 'Shutter Release Project' (www. photovoice.org/shutter-release-picturing-life-after-prison/), which I had previously been involved in evaluating (Loewenthal and Clark 2013). This specific case now described was taken with a group of ex-prisoners with a psychiatric diagnosis who had left prison and were being cared for by the mental health services in an English city where, through the criminal justice system, they were involved with a project to gain employment.

As this was not in a prison setting, there was not the problem so frequently encountered in UK prisons with using cameras, but what is described herein can also be done with Photocards. This pilot project took place over two days (day one: Outlining the process for establishing an action plan to get a job, learning how to use the camera, brainstorming external helps and hindrances, taking photographs and writing captions; day two: Brainstorming internal helps and hindrances, taking photographs, writing captions, force field analysis, and creating an action plan – see Figure 8.1).

Overall, after briefly learning how to use a camera, personal internal and external helps and hindrances in finding a job were identified then explored and modified through a process that involved taking a photograph to represent each help and hindrance. These internal and external forces for and against were then itemised using an approach called 'force field analysis' (Lewin 1943). This enabled participants to focus their energy, as described in the following case of Roger, on that which was most likely to best produce the help they desire by decreasing the forces against, and increase the forces for, getting a job.

Roger

Roger was in his 30s, well-spoken, both keen yet lacking in confidence, and overweight due to psychotropic medication. The focus was to facilitate Roger in getting back into work. Using photographs to help him initially verbalise what he saw as external helps and hindrances (Figure 8.2), followed by internal helps and hindrances (Figure 8.3), he was facilitated to list them and then create a force field analysis,

Rehabilitation and employability: Method

This approach to employability is carried out over two days in the following order and can be done individually or in a group.

Day one

1. Learning how to use the camera.
2. Looking at photographs and critiquing them.
3. Brainstorming external factors that help and external factors that hinder getting a job.
4. Going to take photographs of these external helpful and hindering factors.
5. Returning and critiquing the photographs and considering captions for each of the selected pictures.

Day two

1. Repeating steps 3) to 5) from day one, but for internal rather than external factors that help and hinder getting a job.
2. Each participant drawing a straight line to represent getting a job and then drawing an axis and lists above the straight line all of what s/he considers important external factors for and underneath the line, again going across, all the external factors acting against getting a job.
3. The facilitator helping the participant draw lines pointing downwards for all the relevant forces that are acting externally for getting a job, with the length of each line in proportion to the strength of the force.
4. Similarly, the facilitator helping the participant draw lines up for all the relevant forces that are acting against getting a job.
5. The facilitator then helping the participant determine which force(s) for can be most easily lengthened and then which force(s) against can be most easily reduced.
6. The facilitator enabling the participant to draw up an action plan based on stage 6.
7. Repeating steps 2) to 6) from Day two, this time for internal rather than external factors/forces.

Figure 8.1 Rehabilitation and employability: Method

where the lengths of the lines drawn gave an approximate indication of the strength of the forces for and against his aim of finding a job.

Over the two days, which included walking as a group in the city, talking, and taking photographs, it seemed to become clearer to Roger that he was caught up with various senses of loss, from not completing his academic qualifications to losses in terms of his personal lifestyle, personal relationships, looks, and ability to think and have confidence. Speaking about these ideas seemed to enable Roger to be less clogged up by them. For example, Roger was now able to identify where to put

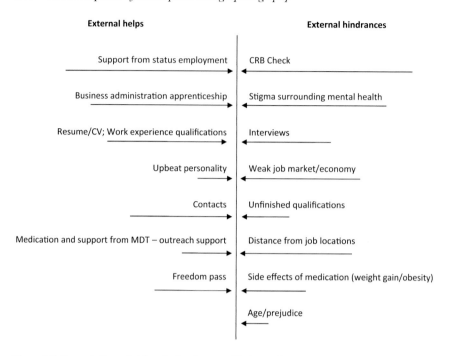

Figure 8.2 Roger's force field analysis of external helps and external hindrances

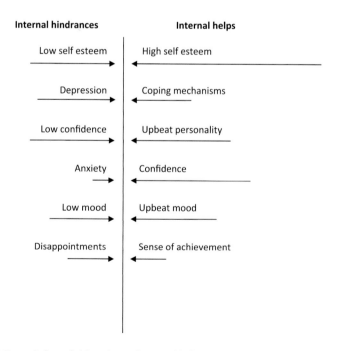

Figure 8.3 Roger's force field analysis of internal helps and internal hindrances

his energies most effectively by choosing the one or two arrows of the 'forces for getting a job' that he could most easily lengthen, and choosing the one or two arrows that represented the 'forces against' that he could most easily shorten. Roger was also able to identify the other forces that he could do little about. Hopefully, by speaking about these forces before, during, and after taking the photographs that characterised them, Roger was then able to work through these 'clogged up' aspects and, in doing so, gain insight into what he should best focus putting his energy into in order to get a job.

Roger decided to prioritise having a contingency plan so that he would change his CV (Figure 8.2) if he didn't get the job he was hoping for (this seemed to show a pragmatism and an ability to overcome potential disappointment). Furthermore, he seemed to realise that there were things he couldn't do anything about, for example, the Criminal Records Bureau (now termed 'Disclosure and Barring Service') check which would show his criminal conviction (Figure 8.2).

When it came to looking at the internal forces by again identifying six helps and six hindrances and then writing a sentence on each before taking photographs and then doing a 'crit', this time Roger only put one word rather than a phrase for each photograph. What came through for Roger was how much all these forces were interconnected, as he said, 'Confidence, mood, esteem – if one is increased or decreased, it affects them all'.

Here, given his concern regarding his coping mechanisms (Figure 8.3), Roger prioritised his need to be able to plan ahead. For example, how long was each aspect of the three-part interview he was about to go for, and what might be asked? (Interestingly, Roger was able to retrieve from the wastepaper basket something on interviewing he had previously done – it was perhaps very much like his story, 'something he had once done well, but had thrown away and was now trying to retrieve'.) On the second day, Roger retold a story of how he had been tricked by a group of friends but ended by saying, 'I earned their respect' whereas previously when he told this story, he just said 'I'd been bullied'.

Something very important that emerged from taking photographs on employability was that Roger was able to recount with growing confidence (as in Figure 8.3) stories regarding how much he had worked in prestigious events and the important people he had met there.

A few weeks later, Roger was selected out of 70 applicants for an apprenticeship training scheme.

Conclusion

The described case of photo-assisted employability/vocational rehabilitation concurs with existing evidence (Falkum et al. 2017) that the majority of persons who are classified as having 'broad schizophrenia spectrum disorders' can cope with some kind of work, given that internal and external barriers are reduced.

The use of force field analysis is just one way that photography can enable individual direct action. It can be seen as a development of a well-established use of photography in this way provided by PhotoVoice (https://photovoice.org/; see also Milne and Muir 2020). In PhotoVoice, individuals and interest groups are trained to use photography to bring about social change. The innovation devised by the author and outlined in this chapter shows participants taking photographs (or using Photocards) to develop action plans. The goals of such personal action plans can vary, for example, from gaining employment (as here and in Loewenthal 2015) to telling one's parents that one is gay (see Chapter 13).

References

Falkum, E. et al. (2017). Vocational rehabilitation for adults with psychotic disorders in a Scandinavian welfare society. *BMC Psychiatry*, 17: 24.

Lewin, K. (1943). Defining the 'field at a given time'. *Psychological Review*, 50: 292–310.

Loewenthal, D. (2015). The therapeutic use of photographs in the United Kingdom criminal justice system. *European Journal of Counselling and Psychotherapy*, 17(1): 39–56.

Loewenthal, D., and Clarke, D. (2013). *Evaluation of PhotoVoice 'Shutter Release Project'*. London: Research Centre for Therapeutic Education, University of Roehampton.

Milne, E., and Muir, R. (2020). Photovoice: A critical introduction. In L. Pauwels and D. Mannay (eds.), *The Sage Handbook of Visual Research Methods*, pp. 282–296. London: Sage. https://dx.doi.org/10.4135/9781526417015.n17.

PhotoVoice. https://photovoice.org/.

Shutter Release Project. http://www.PhotoVoice/shutter-release-picturing-life-after-prison/.

9 The therapeutic use of portraiture (including 'selfies') in the post-truth era

Summary

This chapter explores the use of portraiture, including selfies, as a way of assisting in emotional learning and development. The presentation of 'self' through portraiture with reference to selfies is examined with particular reference to a world with increasing image management and social media. Focus is given to clients exploring what they like and dislike about themselves in photographs and issues for them in accepting what is revealed to them regarding both the positive and negative perceptions of their ageing process through life. A case study is provided together with further considerations of the strengths and limitations in carrying out such approaches, with particular reference to identity and self-image in a post-truth era.

Assignment

Take some selfies. Look at what you consider your worst photograph, one you would normally reject. Write down specifically what each aspect of the way you perceive your look might say about you that you don't want seen. Now, look at what you consider your best photograph. Write down specifically what is it about each aspect of the way you perceive your look and what it might say about you and what you're more ok about others seeing. You can either do this assignment working in pairs and taking turns to take photographs of each other, or do this with 'selfies'.

Key learning points

1. Image management and portraiture have been around for centuries, but with the advent of an increasing focus on identity together with the rise of digital photography and social media, it can be seen as a cultural epidemic.
2. Selfies, like the concept of 'makeovers', can give a person confidence, but can also be an indicator of the desperation to present as who one wants to be rather than who one fears one is.
3. The therapeutic use of portraiture and selfies, as with therapy, can help people accept who they are rather than continuously attempting to produce idealised images.

DOI: 10.4324/9781003240914-10

The therapeutic use of portraiture (including 'selfies')

> Throughout its long history, the self-portrait has been used as a tool to tell
> stories and suggest narratives about who we think we are, who we desire to
> be, how we want others to perceive us, and how we understand ourselves in
> relation to the environments in which we find ourselves at any given time.
>   . . . Self-portraits were and remain a way to try to shape a narrative of
> oneself in the world.
>
> (Okoro 2021)

So, when can portraiture and selfies be helpful and when can they be detrimental?

As Hogan points out in a section entitled 'Selfies and digital realism',

> Mobile-phone technology comes replete with a palate of editing tools to re-
> move imperfections, filters to smooth skin or even make us look thinner.
> A generation of people has grown up with this as a norm and would not con-
> sider posting unedited images of themselves. Indeed, there is great sensitivity
> around what images can be seen on many people's sites and younger women,
> in particular, have internalised the glamorous images.
>
> (Hogan 2022: 54)

In fact, people on Instagram can use the hashtag #nofilter!

> Welcome to the post-truth era – a time in which the art of the lie is shaking
> the very foundations of democracy and the world as we know it. The Brexit
> vote; Donald Trump's victory; the rejection of climate change; the vilifica-
> tion of immigrants; all have been based on the power to evoke feelings and
> not facts.

Thus starts Matthew d'Ancona's (2017) *Post-Truth*, written one year after the
Oxford Dictionary voted 'post-truth' word of the year. So, what of portraiture and
'selfies' in this post-truth era? Does it enable or disenable those involved to distin-
guish feelings from facts?

Questions of truthfulness are not new in the psychological therapies; much has
previously been written about, for example, suggestion masking itself as interpretation (Lacewing 2013; Szasz 1963) and, questioning where recovered memory has
been false memory (Porter et al. 1999).

All this though flies in the face of philosophical traditions where, for example,
for Gadamer (2013), if you want truth you cannot have method. Again, for Levinas
(1961), truth and justice might only occur very rarely between therapist and client,
photographer and photographed (see Chapter 10). Yet, we are also in a /world of
increasingly manualised therapies where the therapeutic use of portraiture if it were
to be regarded as successful would first need to be measured on universal scales –
even at the end of each session! For those trained more traditionally, this may sound

like a joke; but, it is not for those who lose their job if they don't comply and show improvements.

An even greater problem in our post-truth era is the dominant cultural practice termed Cognitive Behavioural Therapy (CBT). I consider that it can be very helpful but it also can be seen to help people take their mind off their problems – an ideological way of denying experience (Loewenthal and Proctor 2018). So, it is all too easy for there to be fewer and fewer opportunities for thoughtful therapeutic practice and any lack of congruence within therapist or client is ignored if not encouraged.

However, importantly on the positive side:

Self-portraiture can be used in a myriad of ways in clinical settings, for instance, in cancer care (Frith and Harcourt 2007), drug dependency centres (Glover-Graf and Miller 2006) and in psychiatric and community settings (Hanieh and Walker 2007), or to explore gender identity (De Oliveira 2003; Wheeler 2020).

(Hogan 2022: 166)

Further, as Okoro (2021) continues:

In our ability to create and take self-portraits that can quickly reach masses of viewers, we have an opportunity to consider how our self-identities intersect with our environment, our countries, our fellow citizens or residents, our collective histories, and our larger sense of wellbeing.

This sounds similar to the continental philosopher Heidegger who writes of us 'being in the world with others' (Heidegger 1962). It can also potentially be seen to be reflected in the 'Self Portrait Experience' work of Cristina Nunez (2013) who considers that this 'is a journey through all aspects of one's life, with a series of artistic exercises, divided in three parts:

• ME: Emotions, character representation, body, places, roots.
• ME AND THE OTHER: One-to-one relationship self-portraits and portraits
• ME AND THE WORLD: Group portraits and self-portraits'

(https://selfportrait-experience.com/the-method/)

Interestingly, Nunez states that the following objectives are for what she claims to be 'the authentic self:

1. To stimulate the unconscious creative process by transforming emotions into artworks.
2. To enrich and empower participants' self-image and perception of themselves.
3. To enrich and empower participants' public image and their perception of others and of society'.

(https://selfportrait-experience.com/the-method/)

Case study: The two hats and what's truthful?

The first panel of Photo 9.1 is a selfie I took on my phone whilst completing this book. But when I got what I took to be a snarky comment about the hat in my family WhatsApp chat, I took and sent the second image in Photo 9.1 with the strap line 'A difficult choice?', to which I got the retort 'So, so hard'. Yet the first image in Photo 9.1 makes me feel narcissistically good. I'm not bothered that I'm the subject, the photographer, and the viewer (Bond et al. 2005); in fact, I'm rather proud of the self-reflection, particularly as I didn't use any filters, Photoshop, etc. It's too easy, though, for me to forget that I chose this photo out of several I took for that shoot. It's even more easy for me to forget how very infrequently I come across such a photo of myself where, at least to myself, I look quite good-looking, with a twinkle in my eye! Yet it must be true that, in reality, other people are far more likely to see me far more similar to all those selfies I bin! Though perhaps that truth is even more reason for attempting to fix, in time, the 'good' self-image!

In the second image in Photo 9.1, the wrinkles and greying hair are more evident, but still the self-parody allows me to at least share it on the family website. But neither of these photographs compares with the intensity of the selfie in Photo 9.2. This was taken when I was about to take, for the first time, the pilot re-enactment photos shown in Chapter 5 with my iPad. My hands were shaking and my whole body felt the enormity and frightening uncertainty of the project I was about to undertake. But could this be what Nunez describes as 'one's higher self'?

Photo 9.1 The two hats

Photo 9.2 Wearing my father's overcoat

The next four photographs were the preliminary shots for me as my father, Louis (Photo 9.3); my grandfather, Eduard (Photo 9.3); my grandmother, Adele (Photo 9.3); and my aunt, Hilde (Photo 9.3). Are these iPad photos what I should have put in the 'Book within a book' of Chapter 5 rather than those studio photos where, whilst I was feeling I had, perhaps appropriately, 'got into being' each of my murdered relatives, the intensity of the anticipatory anxiety was not as present.

Conclusion

Perhaps it could be helpful to learn from Henry James' story *The Real Thing* (James 1893 [2022]). This is where a commercially successful photographer earns his money selling photographs of what appear to be royalty, but are in fact actors (the constructed image, perhaps similar to contrived selfies, let alone 'makeovers'). However, one day, some actual royalty, down on their luck, offer to pose for him. What happens is that soon there is a tension brought about in the taking of the photographs by a photographer telling 'real' royalty how to look, and the photographer subsequently re-engages the actors. The 'royalty', after further unsuccessful employment as the photographer's domestics, are fired. Now, would they have been better photographs if the photographer had photographed the tension with the real royalty – more 'I-Thou' rather than 'I-It' (Buber 1922)? For aren't we also in great danger of being an 'it' and coming even less to our senses with post-truth selfies? Too often attempting to be who we are not rather than at least finding out who we may fear we are?

These points regarding the potential negative aspects of portraiture and selfies can be true of re-enactment phototherapy and therapeutic photography in general. How we portray ourselves and others, previously in family albums, and now on Facebook/Instagram/SnapChat/Tik Tok etc. is an attempt to make permanent the face of ourselves (and of others) that we want remembered. They are probably very

Photo 9.3a *Me as my father*

Photo 9.3b *Me as my father's father*

Photo 9.3c *Me as my father's mother*

Photo 9.3d *Me as my father's sister*

unrepresentative of how others saw us at the time, but the portrait/selfie has the intention of changing that!

On the at least equally important positive side, I return to (Okoro 2021):

What we choose to include in our literal or metaphorical frames, be they glimpses of beauty, symbols of healing, snapshots of nurturing our environment or our community, can all speak to newly reflective narratives we are forming. Narratives that show how we are learning to see ourselves anew, in relation to the people we've been inspired to become, and the selves we're learning to live with after having come through what we have.

References

Bond, A., Woodall, J., Jordanova, L., Clark, T. L., and Koerner, J. L. (2005). *Self Portrait: Renaissance to Contemporary*, Catalogue 224 pages. London: National Portrait Gallery Publications.

Buber, M. (1922). *I and Thou*. New York: Scribner.

D'Ancona, M. (2017). *Post-Truth: The New War on Truth and How to Fight Back*. London: Ebury Press.

De Oliveira, J. B. L. (2003). A mediterranean perspective on the art therapist's sexual orientation. In S. Hogan (ed.), *Gender Issues in Art Therapy*, pp. 126–148. London: JKP.

Frith, H., and Harcourt, D. (2007). Using photographs to capture women's experiences of chemotherapy: Reflecting on the method. *Qualitative Health Research*, 17: 1340–1350.

Gadamer, H. (2013). *Truth and Method*. London: Bloomsbury Academic.

Glover-Graf, N. M., and Miller, E. (2006). The use of phototherapy in group treatment for persons who are chemically dependent. *Rehabilitation Counseling Bulletin*, 49: 166–181.

James, H. (1893 [2022]). *The Real Thing & Other Tales*. London: Moncreiffe Press.

Hanieh, E., and Walker, B. M. (2007). Photography as a measure of constricted construing: The experience of depression through a camera. *Journal of Constructivist Psychology*, 20(2): 183–200.

Heidegger, M. (1962). *Being and Time*. Oxford: Blackwell Publishing.

Hogan, S. (2022). *Photography*. Bingley: Emerald Publishing.

Lacewing, M. (2013). The problem of suggestion in psychoanalysis: An analysis and solution. *Philosophical Psychology*, 26: 718–743.

Levinas, E. (1961). *Totality and Infinity: An Essay on Exteriority*. A. Lingis (trans.). Pittsburgh, PA: Duquesne University Press.

Loewenthal, D., and Proctor, G. (2018). *Why Not CBT?* Wyaston Leys: PCCS Books.

Nunez, C. (2013). The self-portrait as self-therapy. In D. Loewenthal (ed.), *Phototherapy and Therapeutic Photography in a Digital Age*, pp. 95–106. Hove: Routledge.

Okoro, E. (2021). Selfies, self-portraits and our sense of identity. *Financial Times*, 14 August.

Porter, S., Yuille, J. C., and Lehman, D. R. (1999). The nature of real, implanted, and fabricated memories for emotional childhood events: Implications for the recovered memory debate. *Law and Human Behavior*, 23(5): 517–537.

The Self Portrait Experience (SPEX). https://selfportrait-experience.com/the-method/(Accessed 12 September 2022).

Szasz, T. S. (1963). Psychoanalysis and suggestion: An historical and logical analysis. *Comprehensive Psychiatry*, 4(4): 271–280.

Wheeler, M. (2020). Beyond masculine and feminine. In S. Hogan (ed.), *Gender and Difference in the Arts Therapies*, pp. 207–218. Oxon: Routledge.

10 Can phototherapy and therapeutic photography be practices of ethics?

Summary

This chapter explores such questions as: What helps or hinders an exploration of the most effective expressions of phototherapists' and therapeutic photographers' (as well as psychotherapists' and photographers') desire to help? Is it possible to have both justice and action? In examining issues of phototherapy and therapeutic photography as practices of ethics in terms of truth, justice, and responsibility, is there a contemporary ethical basis on which we can assist in an embodied way so that we can help others not do violence to others? Indeed, is it possible for us as phototherapists and therapeutic photographers, (psychotherapists, photographers, etc.) not to interrupt our own and others' continuity, not to play roles in which we no longer recognise ourselves and whereby we betray not only our commitments but our own substance? In particular, what is explored is the question, 'What does it mean then for the person who is the psychotherapist, photographer, etc. to put the person who is the client (or photographed person) first'?

Key learning points

1. Martin Buber's (1922) argument of the difference between an 'I – It' and 'I -Thou' relationship is highly recommended to consider for those involved in phototherapy, therapeutic photography, and all practices involving others.
2. Emanuel Levinas' (1961) argument for the phototherapist or therapeutic photographer (or psychotherapist, photographer, etc.) to be strong enough to put the client/photographer first is also highly recommended for consideration.
3. Appropriate thoughtful practice can be more ethical than an ethical code.
4. The photographer's ethical framework provided in this chapter has been found to be helpful in enabling students and members of other professions such as education, psychological therapies, and management to consider their own ethical practices.

Cases of the ethics of famous photographers

It is argued here that Emanuel Levinas' (1961) notion of ethics as putting the other first transcends previous writings on the ethics of photography and the psychological

DOI: 10.4324/9781003240914-11

therapies. It both opens up the possibility of an ethical dimension within what Rosler (1981) terms 'victim photography' and provides a complementary perspective to, following Sontag (1977), Solomon-Godeau's 'participatory photography' (2003), where the modernistic ethics of Buber (1922) might be more evident.

Thoughts of this chapter emerged on encountering the curator notes at 'The Radical Eye: Modernist photography from the Sir Elton John Collection' (Tate Modern London 10/11/16–21/5/17) stating, 'Evans' captions record the names of his subjects (Walker Evans, Alabama Tenant Farmer, 1936. www.metmuseum.org/art/collection/search/284047), while Lange identified people as representatives of the thousands who shared their plight (Dorothea Lange, Damaged Child, Shacktown, Elm Grove, Oklahoma, 1936. www.moma.org/collection/works/53221)'. I wondered how might one compare the taking of these photographs as ethical practices now as opposed to in the time (1933–1937) of Roosevelt's New Deal? What follows is not a detailed examination of these photographs but the further development (Loewenthal 2022) of what is argued as a prerequisite – a tentative ethical framework for exploring phototherapy and therapeutic photography (and the psychological therapies and photography).

Overall, I wish to explore such vital questions as those raised in the start of this chapter.

In examining such questions, I wish to start by considering whether ethics is separate from practice. If ethics is defined as putting the other first (Levinas 1961), then should we all be striving towards this? An argument here is that ethics is not extraneous to transformative practice. Perhaps to separate ethics from practice is fundamentally unethical? If this is the case, and well-being for others comes before well-being for myself, it has profound implications for the development of phototherapy and therapeutic photography.

What does it mean then for the person who is the photographer 'to put the person who is the photographed first'? Also, what might it mean for the photographed person to appropriately put the photographer 'first'? This form of human relations is very different from that used in our pervading neo-liberal culture of consumer relations, for we may, in putting the other first, have to consider ourselves responsible for the other's responsibility. This may be an important counterbalance to Azoulay's (2008) untethering, through *The Civil Contract of Photography*, of the witnessing photographer from traditional responsibility.

It has been suggested that,

> in the twentieth century, continental philosophers developed a new type of foundation for ethics. . . . A relatively new line of thought made a distinctive relation to other people the central feature of ethics . . . Martin Buber . . . and Emmanuel Levinas are considered the most prominent members of this tradition.
>
> (Becker and Becker 1992: 528–529)

Thus, the inter-subjective theories of ethics of Buber and Levinas are the main focus here, as opposed to other notions of ethics which do not make a distinctive relation to other people the central feature.

However, Buber is a modernist, with the 'I' in the centre, and this I is returned to, such that 'Thou' is seen in relation to the 'I' and that even a claim for distinctness is a difference in relation to the 'I'. Thus, the photographed person is only seen as being different in comparison to something of the photographer. There is always a return to the photographer.

It has been argued that Levinas is postmodern in that we are *subject to* putting the other first (Loewenthal and Snell 2003; Loewenthal 2017). For Levinas, the relation of the photographer to the photographed would define the ethical, but Levinas' 'other' would remain wholly alien and unassimilable. For Levinas, the photographed person's proximity is prior to the photographer's 'presence' and makes it possible, so no totality (a whole that assimilates its parts) can integrate the photographer and photographed. The relation to the photographed person is like a relation to infinity – perpetually beyond experience, making the organising structures of experience possible. It precedes and conditions experience.

As photographers, what then are our values? For Agee, Evans collaborator in *Let Us Now Praise Famous Men*, the camera is 'incapable of recording anything but absolutely dry truth' (1941 [1969]: 206). In contrast, I am assuming that photographers will always be subjective, our values determining how we hear and what we say. That is, in so far as we are able to say what our values are. So, it is vital for our practice that we attempt to consider what we regard as essentially human: Under what circumstances is the world an alive and meaningful place for us as people who are photographers? Is it when we can assertively go after that which appears important to us (autonomy), or does it begin with putting the other first (heteronomy) in a way that recognises the otherness of the other (their alterity)?

In this way, our values and ethics are linked. Levinasian ethics are not therefore about my right to exist or even just about the other's right to exist but can be seen as my responsibility for the other's responsibility to others.

Is photography nothing but relations? It has been suggested that

> photography works with the infinite responsibility that one is never quits with regard to the other. . . . The folds in the photograph demand that we remain responsive to and responsible for the photograph's otherness and its implications of (still) other relations.
>
> (Lomax 1995)

Yet there are deep-seated problems for photography, as Wild (in Levinas 1961: 15) states:

> Totalitarian thinking accepts vision rather than language as its model. It aims to gain an all-inclusive, panoramic view of all things, including the other, in a neutral, impersonal, light. . . . All otherness will be absorbed.

Yet can it ever be possible for a photographer's incorporating vision to also be considerate?

A photographer's ethical window

I devised the 'photographer's ethical window' (see Figure 10.1) as a two-dimensional model; the main axis concerns whether the photographer puts the photographer first or those photographed. The other axis is whether the photographed puts the photographed or the photographer first (The term 'photographed' rather than 'subject' is used to avoid subject-object comparisons here).

In bringing in this second dimension, reciprocity and symmetry are not intended from an individual perspective; however, both dimensions seem needed for responsible relatedness to exist. Again, for the photographer to put the photographed first is a complex notion. It does not necessarily mean doing what the photographed person wants or denying the photographer's desire, as both would not necessarily be putting the other first. There are many other dimensions than those in my frame-up (including that of the photograph's observer and the group the photographed represents), but this window is put forward to focus on the ethical relations between photographer and photographed.

There are two conflicting opinions of Dianne Arbus' book *Untitled* (1995) (www.metmuseum.org/art/collection/search/306263), which incorporates previously unpublished pictures by her of people with developmental disabilities. Some writers (for example, Coleman 1995) refused to review the book, as Arbus did not obtain the consent of those she photographed before photographing them. They assert that the images represent an invasion of privacy. Others (for example, Gross 2012) respond by stating that Arbus behaved reasonably according to the dictates of the time. They outline the danger of censoring photographs by applying anachronistic rules concerning what is acceptable. The Arbus estate, however, compounds the problem by refusing permission to use images to anyone who does not first submit their text to the estate for vetting.

There is, as Sontag (1977) points out, a lack of empathy and identification – Buber's 'I- It'. But this need not necessarily always correlate with Solomon-Godeau's (2003) 'insider/outsider'. Surely one can be an outsider and still take photographs that would or wouldn't, if only at times, be putting the other first (though one could not be certain of knowing this)?

I do not consider Dianne Arbus as putting these particular people first (Diane Arbus Identical Twins, Roselle, NJ, 1967. www.metmuseum.org/art/collection/search/827214), even though it can be argued that such photographs may help in general by making it easier for the public to accept them. I have put them in the (2,2) box, where the 'Photographer puts the Photographer first' and where 'the Photographed puts the Photographer first'. The same could be said of Dorothy

	Photographed puts Photographed first	Photographed puts Photographer first
Photographer puts Photographer first	(2,1) Delahaye	(2,2) Arbus
Photographer puts Photographed first	(1,1) Wearing	(1,2) Bellocq

Figure 10.1 A photographer's ethical window

Lange, where her caption, 'The damage is already done', may bring sympathy for such white children but treats the photographed as an object.

Gillian Wearing's 'Signs that say what you want them to say, and not signs that say what someone else wants you to say' (1992–1993. www.tate.org.uk/art/artworks/wearing-signs-that-say-what-you-want-them-to-say-and-not-signs-that-say-what-someone-else-66092) attempts for the photographer to put the photographed first. However, there is the question of what sort of relationship exists. For Wearing, the relationship is between the person and their slogan, which she states 'interrupts the logic of photo – documentary and snapshot photography by the subjects clear collusion and engineering of their own representation'. (Wearing 1997: 3) But there is also the added complication that Wearing has asked these people to take part in *her* project in the first place. So she does her project, and within it they do theirs. So, I have put her in (1,1) in Figure 10.1.

Wearing opens up the question of 'participatory photography', as described by Rosler (1981), as an antidote to post-colonial incorporation. But this can still be usefully critiqued from a Levinasian perspective. For example, what is our responsibility for what the photographed writes on 'Wearing type' cards or does with the camera we provide?

With the photographs of Luc Delahaye (1999) of people on the Paris metro, what is photographed is that there is not a meeting. The photographer is putting the photographer first in tricking the photographed. The photographed is putting himself/herself first, though does not have the opportunity to take part or not. Baudrillard (1999) says of these photographs,

> No one is looking at anyone else. The lens alone sees but it is hidden. What Delahaye catches then isn't exactly the Other (L'Autre) but what remains of the other, that he, the photographer, isn't there. The ill-assorted gazes of people who see nothing, who are, most importantly, not looking at one another, obsessed as they are with protecting their own symbolic space. Everyone is anonymous and each face vanishes in real time.

However, Baudrillard considers Delahaye's work 'good photography . . . It shows that which is of the order of the inhuman within us'. Thus, it would appear that, for Baudrillard, the aims justify the means.

The notion of relatedness appears unimportant; instead, all are simulations. Thus, the photographer's ethics are unimportant and can be legitimised as 'artistic'. As in Richard Avedon's *What right do Cezanne's apples have to tell Cezanne how to paint them?* (Bolton 1992: 267–268). I have put these photographs by Delahaye as (2,1) in Figure 10.1.

It is Bellocq (E. J. Bellocq, Woman reclining with mask c. 1912; printed c. 1981 from the Storyville Portraits series c. 1911–13. www.ngv.vic.gov.au/explore/collection/work/9173/) who might take the (1,2) position in Figure 10.1 in terms of the ethical window. His photographs of New Orleans sex workers show, I think, a relationship where possibly he is putting the person photographed first, and the person who is photographed is putting him first (whilst one can't be sure, this might be more the intention). As Janet Malcolm states:

> Why Bellocq took these photographs is not known but that they were extraordinary photographs was immediately clear, although the issue of the 'male gaze' – the unpleasant way in which male artists have traditionally scrutinised women's bodies as they painted or sculpted or photographed them – had not yet been raised as such. The friendliness of Bellocq's eye, the reciprocity that flowed between him and his subjects, could not but forcibly strike the viewer . . . Bellocq's mysterious photographs pass the test of good attitude so triumphantly that they seem anachronistic.
>
> (Malcolm 1997: 12)

Even though one of the photographed wears a mask, she looks like she is genuinely enjoying a shared joke and what is captured in the photographed is something of the photographer/photographed relationship.

However, there are also photographs by Bellocq where the face has been violently scratched out (Ernest J. Bellocq, "Storyville Portrait: Woman Standing in front of a Chaise [effaced]" ca 1911–1913. www.moma.org/documents/moma_catalogue_2678_300299020.pdf Last photo). It is not known by whom. Here, as Malcolm points out: 'A mental connection between the savage mark on the plate made by an anonymous hand and the physical abuse that the prostitute is vulnerable to at the hands of strangers is not hard to make' (1997: 15).

This contrasts with how the person becomes objectified and 'subjected to' the photographer's thoughtless violence when the face is obliterated. Perhaps an implication from Levinas is that if the photographer does not obliterate the face of the photographed, then the photographer will have to stay with the responsibility of the other's face, saying 'don't do violence to me'. So did Walker Evans stay with this? Is he also in (1.2) in Figure 10.1? The humanistic way he writes the introduction to *Let Us Now Praise Famous Men* might make one think so. One cannot say they are both in their own worlds (2,1) in Figure 10.1, so is he really similar to Lange? It has been reported that Floyd's son, Charles Burroughs, is still angry at Evans and Agee for not even sending the family a copy of the book and because the family was 'carved in a light that they couldn't do any better, that they were doomed, ignorant' (Whitford 2005). Rosler (1981) is similarly critical of both Lange and Evans. The neutral way Evans captions the photographed with 'Floyd Burroughs Hale County Alabama (1936) Sharecropper' is in contrast to Lange, but is Evans really putting himself first, placing him with Lange in (2,2) Figure 10.1 or is there significantly some more humanity there?

In conclusion, whilst phototherapy and therapeutic photography may not be able to be a complete practice of ethics, I have an idea of whether my intention is putting those I am photographing first. This is within whether I am an insider/outsider (Solomon-Godeau 2003) or attempting participatory photography (Rosler 1981). Whilst Buber can help, Levinas is to be preferred, as difference is more possible, notwithstanding criticisms of Levinas regarding gender (Grosz 1996) and using ethics to escape the rawness of life (Derrida 1996). One implication is that if we only put our concerns first, rather than those of the other, then we are at best privileging a notion of photography that is solely to do with giving a primacy to our autonomy at the expense of others, and our society in general. Perhaps if we are able to face the other as one human being meeting another – even when we are, at least initially, putting ourselves first – we will be more able to, as Levinas implies, do less photographic violence to this other, as I think is the case in Evans' (Walker Evans, Alabama Tenant Farmer 1936) as opposed to Lange's (Dorothea Lange, Damaged Child, Shacktown, Elm Grove, Oklahoma 1936) photographs and captions. Perhaps we all should be more concerned with justice on a case-by-case basis – for from Levinas, real justice in phototherapy and therapeutic photography, even within colonising, cannot be appropriated or territorialised but requires us, from and through our relationships, to be just in the moment with another.

Conclusion

This chapter has explored the use of photography in understanding and developing the ethical place that a phototherapist, therapeutic photographer, psychotherapist, photographer, professional, or artist might take up in relation to another.

Well-known photographs are used in the education of pre- and post-qualifying professionals (and artists) examining with them whether 'photographer' and 'photo-graphed' put either themselves or the other first.

Levinas's notion of ethics as 'putting the other first', is considered more cultur-ally appropriate to the nevertheless vitally important Martin Buber concepts of I/it and I/Thou.

It has been argued that through the exploration of these photographs, ethical face-to-face relationships potentially provide an essential basis for the good.

Without such a relationship, both personally (as explored in therapy), and profes-sionally (as in the education of such professionals as psychological therapists, photog-raphers, teachers, managers, or researchers), there may be far less possibility for truth and justice and a far greater possibility that violence will be done.

The chapter has also given an overview of some criticisms of this use of ethics.

References

Agee, J., and Evans, W. (1941 [1969]). *Let Us Now Praise Famous Men: Three Tenant Families*. Boston: Houghton Mifflin.

Arbus, D. (1967). *Identical Twins*. Roselle, NJ. https://en.wikipedia.org/wiki/Identical_Twins,_Roselle,_New_Jersey,_1967 (Accessed 5 March 2017).

Arbus, D. (1995). *Untitled*. New York: Aperture.

Azoulay, A. (2008). *The Civil Contract of Photography*. New York: Zone Books.

Baudrillard, J. (1999). *L'Autre: Luc Delahaye*. London: Phaidon Press.

Becker, L., and Becker, C. (eds.). (1992). *Encyclopedia of Ethics*. New York: Garland.

Bellocq, E. J. (c. 1911–13a). *Woman Reclining with Mask (c. 1912)*. Printed (c. 1981) from the Storyville Portraits Series. www.ngv.vic.gov.au/explore/collection/work/9173/(Accessed 5 March 2017).

Bellocq, E. J. (c. 1911–13b). *Storyville Portrait: Woman Standing in Front of a Chaise (Effaced)*. www.academia.edu/2318743/Defacement_E._J._Bellocq_and_the_Storyville_Prostitutes (Accessed 5 March 2017).

Bolton, R. (1992). *The Contest of Meaning*. Cambridge, MA: MIT Press.

Buber, M. (1922). *I and Thou*. New York: Scribner.

Coleman, A. (1995). Why I'm saying no to this new Arbus book. *New York Observer*, 9(37): 1, 25, 2 October.

Delahaye, L. (1999). *L'Autre*. Paris: Phaidon. www.artnet.com/magazine/features/sullivan/Images/sullivan4-10-11.jpg (Accessed 5 March 2017).

Derrida, J. (1996). *Archive Fever*. Chicago, IL: Chicago University Press.

Evans, W. (1936). *Alabama Tenant Farmer [Photograph]*. www.metmuseum.org/toah/works-of-art/2000.329/(Accessed 5 March 2017).

Gross, F. (2012). *Diane Arbus's Auguries of Experience*. Minneapolis, MN: University of Minnesota Press.

Grosz, E. (1996). *Space, Time and Perversion – Essays on the Politics of Bodies*. London: Routledge.

Lange, D. (1936). *Damaged Child, Shacktown, Elm Grove, Oklahoma [Photograph]*. www.victoriaolsen.com/tag/dorothea-lange/(Accessed 5 March 2017).

Levinas, E. (1961). *Totality and Infinity: An Essay on Exteriority*. A. Lingis (trans.). Pittsburgh, PA: Duquesne University Press.

Loewenthal, D. (2017). *Existential Psychotherapy and Counselling After Postmodernism: The Selected Works of Del Loewenthal*. Abingdon: Routledge.

Loewenthal, D. (2022). Chapter 12, the ethics of the relational. In D. Loewenthal (ed.), *Levinas and the Other in Psychotherapy and Counselling*. London: Routledge.

Loewenthal, D., and Snell, R. (2003). *Post-Modernism for Psychotherapists: A Critical Reader*. Hove: Brunner-Routledge.

Lomax, Y. (1995). Folds in the photograph. *Third Text*, 9: 32, 43–58.

Malcolm, J. (1997). The real thing. *New York Review*, 6 January.

Rosler, M. (1981). Around and afterthoughts. In R. Bolton (ed.), *The Contest of Meaning*. Cambridge, MA: MIT Press.

Solomon-Godeau, A. (2003). Winning the game when the rules have been changed: Art photography and postmodernism. In L. Wells (ed.), *The Photography Reader*, pp. 152–163. London: Routledge.

Sontag, S. (1977). *On Photography*. London: Penguin Books.

Tate Modern Exhibition. (2016–2017). *The Radical Eye: Modernist Photography from the Sir Elton John Collection*, 10 November–21 May. www.tate.org.uk/whats-on/tate-modern/radical-eye-modernist-photography-sir-elton-john-collection (Accessed 12 September 2022).

Wearing, G. (1992–1993). *From: Signs That Say What You Want Them to Say and Not Signs That Say What Someone Else Wants You to Say, 'I'm Desperate'*. www.accaonline.org.au/sites/default/files/styles/acca_event_header/public/header_image/1440_gillian.jpg?itok=Y0Y-PU4K (Accessed 5 March 2017).

Wearing, G. (1997). *Signs That Say What You Want Them to Say and Not Signs That Say What Someone Else Wants You to Say 1992–1993*. London: Interim Art.

Whitford, D. (2005). The most famous story we never told. *Fortune Magazine*, 19 September.

Wild, J. (1961). Introduction. In E. Levinas (ed.), A. Lingis (trans.), *Totality and Infinity: An Essay on Exteriority*, pp. 11–20. Pittsburgh, PA: Duquesne University Press.

11 Phototherapy and therapeutic photography

Theories, research, and evaluation

Summary

This chapter gives an overview of approaches to theory, research, and evaluation in phototherapy and therapeutic photography. A case study is then provided of the use of theory and research in evaluating the therapeutic effectiveness of Talking Pictures Therapy in the context, as referred to in Chapter 2, of working in schools. The focus is on photographs used in brief psychotherapy and counselling with the purpose of enabling clients to express and explore aspects of their lives they would like to talk about. The author presents examples using Talking Pictures Therapy in brief therapy with children aged 12 to 14 years old in a UK school setting. The use of photographs is discussed further as an evaluative measure in assessing the client's 'progress' through their choice and resulting descriptions of the photographs chosen, as compared with standardised measures of client progress.

Key learning points

1. Start by trying to identify your *research question* in one simple sentence. It might be focussing on practice, theory, or empirical research, and its purpose might be exploratory, descriptive, or causal.
2. Carry out a *literature review* of the key word or words in the research question (this could include the definitions of concepts, and/or the assumptions made, and/or the methods used of any related empirical research and their findings).
3. Besides Google Scholar and other search engines, https://phototherapy-centre.com/who-is-doing-what-where/ can be a useful resource.
4. Explore *methodological issues* and what leads to the selection of a particular research method.
5. Describe the particular *research method* chosen (it could be a quantitative, qualitative, or mixed methods), how the sample of research participants was selected, and what information they were provided with.
6. Describe the *ethical* approval process you adopted.
7. Provide the *analysis* of your results.
8. Give your *conclusions*, and explain how these conclusions compared with other research findings and what suggestions you have for further research.

DOI: 10.4324/9781003240914-12

9. The earlier stages (which are adhered to more closely in empirical research) may be presented under similar headings in a research report but in practice represent *an iterative process* whereby each stage, when considered in relation to another, can lead to modifications.

10. Besides *methodological* issues concerning method, research is frequently concerned with issues of knowledge (*epistemology*) and of being (*ontology*).

11. Thus, regarding epistemology, there are questions about *the nature of phototherapy and therapeutic photography knowledge* (for example, the extent to which such knowledge is explicit or tacit).

12. Regarding ontology, there are such questions as to the *assumptions about being human* that various therapeutic modalities/schools of psychology make. Such assumptions could include whether one sees people as fundamentally good or evil, free or determined, rational or irrational, etc. and perhaps the resulting humanistic emphasis on *feelings*, or psychoanalytic emphasis on an *unconscious*, or existential emphasis on *experience*, or behavioural emphasis on *cognition*, etc.

Exercise

Either: Choose a photograph (from the Talking Picture Cards or another set) before the commencement of a phototherapeutic intervention. (The therapeutic intervention could also be counselling/psychotherapy or anything else that might be therapeutic, for example going on holiday, meeting people, doing or taking part in something artistic, working, etc.). Now, write about why you chose that photo/what it brings to mind regarding your experiences, moods, feelings, thoughts, etc.

When the (photo)therapeutic intervention has been completed, choose another photograph and again write about why you chose that photo/what it brings to mind regarding your experiences, moods, feelings, thoughts, etc. Next, look at the two before and after descriptions and write down any differences/changes in your experiences, moods, feelings, thoughts, etc.

Or: More traditionally (though the involvement of a qualified psychological therapist is even more encouraged) self-administer the PHQ-9 and GAD-7 (available online) for depression and anxiety, both before and then after the phototherapy or therapeutic photography intervention. Observe if there are any differences in the before and after scoring.

You could also do both of these alternatives and compare any differences in the findings.

Researching phototherapy and therapeutic photography

Research can be considered a cultural practice (fashioning culture and being fashioned by it). Definitions of research therefore change, as, for example, in the case of the body assessing UK university research, which has defined research as 'a process of investigation leading to new insights, effectively shared' (REF 2014). Yet, this body's forerunner defined it as 'an original investigation undertaken in order to gain knowledge and understanding' (RAE 2008). There are many alternative definitions, such as '[an] attempt to find out information in a systemic manner' (Princeton Wordnet Web 2006), etc.

Psychotherapeutic research has, as of late, been involved in examining processes and outcomes with an increasing interest from governments and the professions in so called 'evidence-based practice'. There exists an abundance of qualitative and quantitative approaches to psychotherapeutic research, though all have their limitations. Rather, the position is seriously considered here, as can be argued with psychotherapy (Lees and Freshwater 2008), that phototherapy and therapeutic photography practice itself is the research. Hence, the psychological therapies are their own research methods, for the origin of their approach, physis, is what comes out of itself, and therefore external research methods can bring force to bear which can sometimes be violent (Loewenthal 2016).

Qualitative and quantitative research

Quantitative research is more associated with 'positivism' and is concerned with counting and measuring things, producing in particular estimates of averages and differences between groups, whereas qualitative research is more associated with being 'interpretative' and has its roots in social science and is more concerned with understanding why people behave as they do: Their knowledge, attitudes, beliefs, fears, etc.

One of the aims of positivistic research is to discover natural and general laws and to enable people to predict and control events. This type of research generally assumes that reality is objectively given and can be described by measurable properties which are independent of the researcher. Conversely, interpretative research methods are designed to help researchers understand people and the social/cultural contexts within which they live by describing meaningful interactions.

There is an argument that what may now be required is that phototherapy and therapeutic phototherapy be subjected to randomised control trials (RCTs), although the use of RCTs is increasingly questionable for exploring the effectiveness of psychological therapies in general (Guy et al. 2012). RCTs are, however, still regarded as the main legitimising instruments in our current dominant culture.

An interesting and important development is in the field of visual research. However, it is still often only seen as an adjunct to more traditional existing research methods (see, for example, Banks 2001). There is also the question of whether there is a particular need for qualitative research on the therapeutic use of photographs in a similar way to that now being conducted in counselling and psychotherapy, where approaches are used to aggregate primarily qualitative data from interviews using such methods as grounded theory, phenomenological research, discourse analysis, heuristic research, case study methods, etc. (see, for example, Loewenthal 2007; Loewenthal and Winter 2007).

Phototherapy, however, provides the opportunity to consider not only these traditional research approaches but also the growing field of visual research.

What is visual research?

As has previously been mentioned, the key argument running throughout this chapter is that the practices of phototherapy and therapeutic photography, as with psychotherapy, are synonymous with the practice of research. However, it is also considered important to consider possible implications of developments in related areas such as visual research.

Visual research uses both researcher-created data and respondent-created data, which could be compared with phototherapy and therapeutic photography respectively. A prominent visual method is the use of photo elicitation, which would appear similar to projective techniques of phototherapy. However, visual research is still considered a rather dispersed and ill-defined domain (Prosser 2006).

According to Banks (Banks 2001; Pauwels 2011), there are three main strands to visual research in the social sciences:

- Found materials (social scientists as image collectors)
- Researcher-initiated productions (social scientists as image creators)
- Participatory productions (social scientists as the participatory facilitators)

Banks (2001) advises that visual research methodologies should only be used as part of a more general package of research methodologies and the need for them should be indicated by the research itself. Whilst psychotherapeutic researchers try and identify the research questions that lie behind the specific investigation, visual research methodologies are often used in an exploratory way to discover what the researcher has not initially considered. This can be seen in terms of 'making the familiar strange and hence more perceptible' (Mannay 2010).

It is also important to note that the meaning of images changes over time as they are viewed by different audiences. Similarly, the meaning intended by the phototherapeutic researcher when creating the image may not be the meaning that is read by the viewer. (Photographs are also used differently by phototherapeutic researchers who adopt either a positivistic or interpretative approach.)

Questions for the researcher carrying out research into phototherapy or therapeutic photography

Here are some further questions the phototherapeutic researcher might find useful to hold in mind:

- Who is the researcher?
- Is the client the researcher?
- Is the phototherapist the researcher?
- Is it collaborative research?
- Should the phototherapist be a practitioner researcher?
- Should the researcher be independent of all of the roles described here?
- What is the reason for the research?
- Is the researcher interested in a positivistic or interpretative approach to research?

It would appear vital, therefore, that phototherapeutic researchers need both to make clear their position and have thought about these questions before the research is carried out.

Examples of possible small-scale research projects within phototherapy and therapeutic photography

There is now an urgent need for research to be carried out on phototherapy and therapeutic photography, not only in terms of neuroscience and, if the funding is available, in terms of RCTs (despite their limitations) but also in terms of the considerable practice-based research of professional postgraduate psychological therapy training programmes. Examples of the potentially infinite number of research project areas could include:

- The representation of experience in phototherapy, with particular reference to mothers of children with a significant language delay.
- Questioning the phototherapist as a practitioner researcher: Asking questions in the therapeutic hour.
- The phototherapists' experience of working with despair in a UK prison setting.
- Exploring the experience of phototherapist trainee working in organisations offering a time-limited service.
- Exploring phototherapists' experience of medical model thinking when working in both primary care and private practice.

In considering the relative merits of quantitative, qualitative, and visual research, an example is now provided of research carried out to evaluate phototherapy as part of counselling and psychotherapy.

Research case: Talking Pictures Therapy as brief therapy in a school setting

I would now like to present one example of a comparison of quantitative, qualitative, and visual research where photographs have been used as part of counselling and psychotherapy.

Talking Pictures Therapy is an approach to brief therapy and counselling in which photographs are used to help clients express and explore aspects of their lives. This section provides more context and exploration of the research of which the case of Amanda, described in Chapter 2, was part. Here, reference is also made through brief case vignettes to the use of Talking Pictures Therapy with three other children, ages 12 to 14 years, in this pilot study in a UK school setting.

The purpose of this 'collective case study' was to explore and, in turn, evaluate this Talking Pictures Therapy, which is the name the author has given to the use of photographs within psychotherapy and counselling. The therapeutic work, which forms the data of this study, was carried out in a UK school. The four children (Key Stage Three to Key Stage Four) were informed that Talking Pictures Therapy normally involved up to six sessions of one-on-one therapy with the purpose of enabling them to express and explore, in the therapy and potentially through photographs, aspects of their lives they would like to talk about.

Theoretical overview

Within the field of therapy, phototherapy and therapeutic photography are not completely separate entities but may be classified as existing on the continuum of photo-based healing practices. The two practices involve making use of the 'emotional-communication qualities of photographs and people's interactions with them' (Weiser 2004: 1) to enable clients to speak of difficulties they experience (Weiser 1999, 2001). Phototherapy and therapeutic photography were mainly developed in the 1980s and 1990s (Krauss and Fryrear 1983; Spence 1986; Walker 1986; Weiser 1999).

Given what might be currently termed as 'the digital era', there appears to be a recent resurgence of interest in phototherapy and therapeutic photography (Loewenthal 2011; Weiser 2000). This revival has been spurred by the advent of camera phones and increasingly inexpensive digital cameras, along with the availability of the internet enabling easy access to images on social networking sites such as Facebook and YouTube (Loewenthal 2013). Phototherapy, as described in Chapter 1, is the use of photographs to enable clients' expression of their concerns (Krauss and Fryrear 1983; Weiser 2002), whereas therapeutic photography often involves self-initiated, photo-based activities conducted by a person, not necessarily a therapist, who guides the experience for self-exploration and personal growth (Martin and Spence 1987, 1988; Spence 1986). This process often entails taking photographs to work through an emotional constriction. The distinctions between phototherapy and therapeutic photography are not always clear, and some practitioners use the methods interchangeably within their practice.

Photographs can be a route to the unconscious mind via the meaning clients attach to them. These projections may represent repressed feelings or experiences. Repression is an unconscious exclusion of memories, impulses, desires, and thoughts that are too difficult or unacceptable to deal with in consciousness. Freud believed that 'the essence of repression lies simply in turning something away and keeping it at a distance from the conscious' (1915: 147). Photographs may be a device through which clients repressions can be realised. Similarly, Weiser (2001) discussed photo-projective methods in which clients project meaning onto photographs. The photograph may act as a tool, helping the client to become aware of their interpretation of the world. When incorporated into therapy, photographs have been reported to be effective at facilitating improvements with impulse control, social skills, and self-esteem. Furthermore, photographs can be useful as a metaphor for the self, allowing the therapist to enter the client's experience of reality while enabling the client to form more realistic concepts of themselves (Phillips 1986). Comfort (1985) introduced clients to the value of visual language as a foundation for imagery communication between the client and the therapist.

Talking Pictures Therapy as brief therapy with children

Defined as the use of photographs within brief counselling and psychotherapy, Talking Pictures Therapy is a process that can be incorporated into any psychological therapy. Talking Pictures Therapy aims to enable the client to speak of their concerns within such approaches as humanistic, existential, and psychoanalytic/psychodynamic therapy (Loewenthal 2011).

With regard to short-term, psychodynamic psychotherapy, several studies have evaluated its effectiveness for children and adolescents. Muratori et al. (2002) evaluated brief psychodynamic psychotherapy for children with anxiety or depression and found that the children increased in global social functioning. These results are similar to those of Horn et al. (2005), who found that short-term psychoanalytic psychotherapy for the treatment of depression in children and adolescents led to decreases in depression scores. However, Christogiorgos et al. (2010) highlighted potential limitations of the use of psychodynamic brief therapy with children, including children's initial struggles in communication and difficulties in expressing thoughts and feelings.

Encouragingly, the use of photographs in therapy is particularly effective with children who struggle to articulate themselves emotionally but respond powerfully to visual images (Loewenthal 2009). In particular, research on the use of photographs with children in school settings has been reported to facilitate the enhancement of self-concept and lead to improvements in mind-state and emotional management (Halkola and Koffert 2011). Talking Pictures Therapy is introduced as a method for promoting well-being in children and can be carried out by psychotherapists or other mental health professionals who have at least some basic therapeutic training. When using Talking Pictures Therapy in schools, teachers and those such as SENCOs, in the UK, should not be assumed to have received such training.

Researchers report that the use of photographs in therapy enables secondary school–aged children to experience improvements with social skills (Loewenthal 2011) and self-esteem (Sponseller 1979). Phototherapy was found to lead to improvements in mind-state and emotional management in school children in Finland (Halkola and Koffert 2011), as well as to enable children in Italy to experience a more positive identity (Loewenthal 2010), resulting in the potential for reductions in depression and anxiety.

Participants

The four children attended a school on the south coast of England in an area of relative deprivation and ranged between 12–14 years in age. The local community and, in turn, the school, was made up of a large proportion of white, working-class children with some children from Eastern Europe and Southeast Asia. The school was a secondary with attached sixth form. This school, through the SENCO, prioritised four children for Talking Pictures Therapy. These children, with permission of their parents/guardians, agreed to receive the therapy and for it to be used for this research.

Method

Qualitative and quantitative methods, alongside using the children's choice of photographs in terms of visual research, were used. With regard to qualitative research, a case study method was utilised as a research approach based on Greenwood and Loewenthal (2005, 2007), where Husserlian bracketing is combined with hermeneutics, strongly influenced by Bleicher's (1980) work on the phenomenology of Heidegger (1962) and Gadamer (2013). We, in turn, developed this further from Yin's (1984) consideration of the case study method as a means of generalisation. A collective case study sample including four children was chosen on Yin's (2014) recommendation that conclusions are often considered stronger in multiple case analyses than in single case study analysis.

The case study method sought to reveal multiple meanings by a process of searching and then re-searching the therapist's account of the therapy. This research followed the four stages of a phenomenological-hermeneutic case study method (Greenwood and Loewenthal 2005), where the number of stages depends on the amount of 're-searching' for meanings that take place and where there is no limit to this part of the process.

The case study emerges as a consequence of following the stages outlined in Figure 11.1 and represents the final stage of the method. A suitable quantitative

---

Stage one

Begin with the therapy that forms the basis of the observation.

Stage two

A therapist makes a written account of what took place in a session soon after the meeting (preferably directly afterwards).

Stage three

These early reflections are subject to the considerable influence of the therapist's 'pre-understandings', perhaps in terms of their cultural background and gender, that are inherent in any account of human observation. The therapist's supervisor can exert a potential influence by being involved in a process of reflection on the data from the sessions. At this stage, the initial data will have been subject to a re-interpretation, allowing for additional meanings to emerge from the influence of the 'pre-understandings'.

Stage four

The researcher will subject this therapeutic account to further scrutiny when writing up these findings in the form of a report providing a further opportunity for meanings to emerge and the possibilities to be explored.

Figure 11.1 Phenomenological-hermeneutic case study method

assessment set was also used: PHQ-9 (for depression), GAD-7 (for anxiety), the Improving Access to Psychological Therapies (IAPT) Phobia Scale (IAPT minimum data set), and the popular overall measure CORE-10. (These were assumed to be the most common methods currently used to evaluate therapeutic effectiveness in the UK.)

The author also wished to consider the 'progress' of the therapy through client's choice of photographs and the individual meanings projected onto them.

Participants and sampling

Two further case examples (to the one in Chapter 2 of the four children in this study) are now provided. Both children attended this school on the South coast of England, which is in an area of relative deprivation. The children were 12 and 13 years old, respectively. The local community, and thus the school, was made up of a large proportion of white children from working-class families, with some children from Eastern Europe and Southeast Asia. The school was a secondary school with an attached sixth form.

The school, through their Special Education Needs Coordinator (SENCO), prioritised four children for the Talking Pictures Therapy. These children, with permission of their parents/guardians, agreed to receive the intervention and allow outcomes to be used for research purposes. Some descriptions have been changed to protect confidentiality. The children were seen at their school once a week for 50 minutes each session for up to six sessions.

Process description

Talking Pictures Therapy is the use of photographs (or Photocards) in brief counselling and psychotherapy. Within Talking Pictures Therapy, each child was asked to select a photograph in the initial and final session, as well as at other appropriate or useful times in the therapy. The selection of photographs used for this study was Spectrocards, an associative set of 60 Photocards created for practitioners to use within therapeutic activities.

Spectrocards are claimed to 'facilitate sharing in counselling through captivating imagination, exposing feelings, and promoting storytelling' (Halkola 2013).

Evaluative process

The photographs chosen by the children were considered a measure of their progress. Evaluative data (see Figure 11.2) were collected in the initial and final sessions with each child, using the main elements of the IAPT Phobia Scale, the GAD-7, the PHQ-9, and the CORE-10.

These are the most common methods currently used to evaluate therapeutic effectiveness in the UK. The GAD-7 is most commonly used as a self-administered patient questionnaire and as a screening tool and severity measure for

Evaluative measurement tool	Scores	Charlotte	Winston	Linda	Amanda
GAD-7	Pre	9	0	2	4.5
(Anxiety)	Post	9	0	0	4
PHQ-9	Pre	13	5	2	5
(Depression)	Post	8	7	0	4
CORE-10	Pre	11	8	8	12
	Post	9	14	4	6

Figure 11.2 GAD-7, PHQ-9, and CORE-10 pre- and post-scores

generalised anxiety disorder. The PHQ-9 is used to monitor the severity of depression and response to treatment; it is claimed that it can be used to make a tentative diagnosis of depression (Barkham et al. 2012). CORE-10 is a session-by-session monitoring system to be used as a screening tool and outcome measure. The assessments were coded through the standard coding set for these quotients and were completed by an independent coder. Due to the phenomenological approach of this study, validity and reliability were not considered viable concepts.

In both case examples, an effort was made to expand upon the children's choice of photograph, while illustrating the use of Talking Pictures Therapy as an approach to brief therapy with children. The case examples will also consider photographs as an evaluative tool in assessing the progress of the therapy through the client's choice of photographs and the individual meanings projected onto them, in comparison with the quantitative assessment set: PHQ-9, GAD-7, and the main elements of the IAPT Phobia Scale and CORE-10.

With regard to evaluating the effectiveness of Talking Pictures Therapy, alongside the descriptions from the clients of their chosen photograph, quantitative measures were recorded at the beginning and end of each client's course of therapy.

Results

Case examples: Charlotte and Winston

Charlotte: Photographs as process and outcome

Charlotte was 12 years old when she came for six sessions of Talking Pictures Therapy at her school. She had an engaging and soulful air about her. At the start of the phototherapy, Charlotte said the photo she chose had a 'twist' in it (Photo 11.1a). She said she found it difficult to talk about her situation because her father had been run over and killed three years before, and her mother had never wanted to know her. She lived with her paternal grandmother and aunt. Her aunt had been in psychiatric hospitals from age 16, after being in foster care, and was in crime.

Photo 11.1a A twist

Photo 11.1b Trees and green leaves

Charlotte talked about films and said her favourite was a story in which 10 peo-ple were killed in a Range Rover in Africa but no one was sure if the person taken prisoner did it or not. She disclosed that her father had been involved in some criminal activity, but that it did not necessarily mean there was not any good in him. Charlotte seemed relieved when I said there could be both good and bad in everybody. Charlotte's 15-year-old brother, whom she didn't know very well, was currently in custody. She also had a sister in foster care whom she had hardly ever seen, but with whom she was hoping to reconnect through her brother. I later discovered that this sister lived near Charlotte's school, but Charlotte did not know which house number. Charlotte worried what reception she would receive if she sought her sister out.

Charlotte revealed that her brother was in prison because he got another boy to hold somebody down while he threatened him with a knife. Charlotte said, in a dis-believing voice, 'The boy who had been threatened claimed that his face was black-and-blue, but it could not have been so'. Together, Charlotte and I wondered if she took on the values of her family, who is notorious for crime in the area. However, crime was something Charlotte had said she did not want to get into. Charlotte told me that her favourite subject was drama, and that the other children were impressed at how realistically she was able to play the part of a drug dealer. 'More crime,' I said, and she looked crestfallen.

In the fifth session, I again asked Charlotte to choose a photograph that called to her. The Spectrocard she chose had some trees and green leaves on it (Photo 11.1b).

She said it reminded her of a peaceful place she goes to where there is nobody else. She described it as a lane, and though someone had been murdered further down the road, her peaceful spot was safe, 'but I suppose one has to be careful'. In the last session, she brought in a photograph of the trees in the lane that she had taken on her mobile phone.

PHQ-9, GAD-7, and CORE-10 (see Figure 11.2)

The PHQ-9 showed the greatest movement, with a beginning score of 13 (indicating moderate depression) and a final score of 8 (indicating mild depression). At the end of Charlotte's sessions, there was a significant shift regarding whether she had 'little pleasure or interest in doing anything during the previous two weeks.

Charlotte's answer changed from 'nearly every day' to 'not at all', and she said that she was more engaged in 'doing things' and was going out more. Regarding her appetite (the scale item covers 'poor appetite' or 'overeating'), her scores moved from 'more than half the day' to 'not at all'. Showing that her clothes no longer fit, she said that she didn't feel the need to keep eating now. Regarding the item 'being fidgety', she now replied 'not at all' as opposed to 'more than half the day', as in the initial evaluation.

Her score at the GAD-7 remained unchanged between the beginning and the end of the sessions of Talking Pictures Therapy. She scored 9 both times, where 5 and 10 are indicated as mild anxiety and moderate anxiety, respectively.

Regarding the CORE-10 measure, Charlotte scored 11 at the commencement of therapy and 9 at the end. A score of 11 or greater is regarded as being in the clinical range and in the lower boundary of the mild clinical level. One positive change was found on the CORE-10 measure; at the end of therapy, Charlotte reported that during the past week, 'unwanted images and memories' had been distressing her 'only occasionally', whereas at the start of therapy, she had seen them as 'occurring often'. She did, however, report difficulty in getting to sleep from previously 'only occasionally' to 'constant', primarily because she had been sleeping in a chair in the living room with her Gran, while her aunt slept in the bedroom.

Overview

It seemed as if Talking Pictures Therapy enabled Charlotte to reduce her depression and talk more about her anxieties. She was able to find places outside the therapy session to do more with her friends and on her own. Although she did not want to be involved in crime, for which her mother's and father's families are infamous; she needed to talk about it.

Winston: Photographs as process and outcome

Winston was a 13-year-old Black boy who I had been told was almost mute, and at the first meeting, he appeared to be obedient but did not want to speak. When Winston did talk, it was in a quiet whisper. The first photograph he chose was of

Photo 11.2a Catherine wheel   *Photo 11.2b* Noughts and crosses   *Photo 11.2c* Playing cards

a Catherine Wheel (Ferris wheel) at a fairground (Photo 11.2a), which he said reminded him of when he went to a fair with his parents and two sisters the previous summer. It appeared that he sometimes played at home with his sisters, but not with his parents.

At the next meeting, Winston was asked to choose another photograph that called to him. This time he chose one with noughts and crosses (Photo 11.2b), which he said, whispering, that he enjoyed playing with his sisters. Winston and I played noughts and crosses together for about 20 minutes. I then asked him if he would like to play another game called 'Connect 4'. Winston was very interested in this and soon became proficient at the game. While playing Connect 4, I told him I had noticed during the pre-therapy evaluation questions that he had chosen the response 'sometimes' for the statement, 'Over the past week, I have made plans to end my life'. I wondered what had made him say that. Winston confessed, in a whisper, that Linda (another child at his school also taking part in Talking Pictures Therapy) told him she did not like him because of the colour of his skin, and he said she hit him and insulted him and his family. I offered to speak to the staff about this. He nodded vigorously.

At the start of the next session, Winston wanted to play Connect 4 again. When asked if the other student had stopped bullying him, Winston nodded with a happy smile on his face, whispering, 'Yes'. After two more games, I asked him if he'd always spoken quietly. 'No', he said faintly in my ear. When I asked when he started speaking only in a whisper, he replied, 'I was 5' and resumed the game.

At the following session, Winston appeared more relaxed and was more engaging. He chose to play a game I had introduced to him in one of the sessions, Scrabble. While we were playing, I said to him that I had wondered what happened to him at the age of 5, when he stopped talking. Winston seemed unable to even whisper, so I said, if he wanted to, he could write it down. He wrote, 'My mother tell me to stop talking two [sic] . . . much, and I stopped talking'. I asked him if he would like to talk more, and when he nodded; I wondered aloud how we could help him.

In the penultimate session, I asked Winston if he would like to choose another photograph that called to him, and he chose one depicting playing cards (Photo 11.2c). When asked why he chose that card, Winston replied, 'My mother used to play cards in Africa, before we came here a year ago'. He told me that he no longer played with his mother, who also does not speak very much. I asked if it was common that the women of the same age as his mother did not talk very much in that African country. Winston looked at me, amused and smiling, shook his head as if I was a bit stupid, and then made me understand that he wished to carry on playing Scrabble.

At the start of the sixth and last session, I asked Winston if he wanted to play games or to talk, and surprisingly, his response was, 'Talk'. Then, hesitantly and quietly, he said that he had been thinking that while his mother does not talk, this was not the same for his mother's sister. He also told me in the course of the same session that he played tennis with his mother after telling her that he wanted to become a tennis player. Smiling, he also told me that he had a friend now with whom he plays at school.

PHQ-9, GAD-7, and CORE-10 (see Figure 11.2)

Winston scored 5 on the PHQ-9 scale measuring depression at the start of therapy and 7 at the end of his last session. The primary change was that he now felt he had trouble concentrating. This indicated mild-to-moderate depression. On the GAD-7 scores, which measure anxiety, he scored 0 both pre-therapy and post-therapy. Regarding the CORE-10, his initial score was 8, and his final score was 14. Changes included an increase in 'feeling depressed or unhappy', though he did now feel that he had 'someone to turn to for support'.

Overview

In the course of the six sessions, Winston seemed to have changed from being described by his teachers as an 'elective mute', to a young boy who was now able, according to staff, to look at and speak to people. It could be that the increase in CORE-10 scores was a result of the new ability to voice what was of concern to him.

Discussion

Within work with children, the Talking Pictures Therapy approach seemed to provide a useful way of opening up a therapeutic encounter by enabling the therapy to quickly access the client's concerns. Charlotte initially chose a photo that could be seen to have indicated her turbulent state of mind – the metal with the twist in it. This action supports the particular effectiveness of the use of photographs in therapy with children who struggle to articulate themselves emotionally (Loewenthal 2010).

It can be concluded that at the end of therapy, Charlotte chose photographs that may indicate she had found a safer place from which to speak, a lane with some trees where Charlotte could be on her own. For Winston, the Talking Pictures Therapy enabled him to find his voice. He began by holding on to the precious memory of playing with his sisters but was eventually able to voice, through the picture of the playing cards, his experience of his mother telling him not to speak, as well as her own choice to speak infrequently. Allowing the clients to choose their own photographs enabled them to manage their own therapy.

These findings may further support previous research, which reported that use of photographs in therapy leads to improvements, as previously mentioned, with social skills (Loewenthal 2011), self-esteem (Sponseller 1979), and mind-state and emotional management in children (Halkola and Koffert 2011).

In many ways, within the Talking Pictures Therapy, it may be considered that the children were able to begin to work through what might be considered an emotional constriction, enabling them to find a voice and safer places to be. It is considered here that photographs may be seen as a route to the unconscious with the working-through of the child's projections, enabling an opportunity through which emotional learning took place. Importantly, it was found within this study that Talking Pictures Therapy as a form of brief therapy enabled children to speak of their concerns and seemed not to suffer from the limitations posed by brief psychodynamic therapy with children, within which the children are often challenged with communicating and expressing their concerns (Christogiorgos et al. 2010).

It is important to note that there are, nevertheless, some potential disadvantages to a Talking Pictures Therapy. The first is that clients might be so comfortable speaking about their problems that the ability to manage the problem's representation in the photograph may not come easily. The second concern is whether photographs or projective techniques (in a digital era where photographs are so commonplace) could be used consciously or unconsciously to make one person carry out another's agenda. It is therefore recommended that Talking Pictures Therapy be carried out by a therapist who has at least some basic therapeutic interpersonal training, which also involves the therapist gaining personal insight. In particular, teachers and SENCOs should not be assumed to have these abilities (even though many will have gained some of these abilities through their work experience).

With regard to the evaluative data measures (see Figure 11.2), following the Talking Pictures Therapy, Charlotte saw a decrease in depression as measured by the PHQ-9 score between pre-therapy and post-therapy evaluation, alongside a decrease in the CORE-10 clinical range score. Winston's scores, both PHQ-9 and CORE-10, show an increase between pre- and post-therapy. However, it is felt that the score may have increased because the therapy had enabled Winston to speak of what was troubling him. However, both clients appeared to respond more thoughtfully to CORE-10 than to PHQ-9 or GAD-7, perhaps because CORE-10 was the last questionnaire and it was possible that they had gained more practice in thinking about the questions.

In turn, there was also the feeling of a further violence against the client, for example in asking clients to respond to such questions as whether they have made plans to end their life and then moving onto the next question. This effect appears to be mitigated when questionnaires are followed by therapy evolving through a human relationship. (But wouldn't no questionnaires be even better - see below?)

Using photographs in a therapeutic context appears not only to support the therapeutic dialogue based on client's projections but can also be used as a more descriptive device for the evaluation of the therapy outcome. For example, Charlotte's starting with photographs indicating her turbulent state of mind and, during the course of the brief therapy, choosing a photograph indicating a calmer place showed progress made throughout the therapy. It is important to consider phototherapy as a different method of research.

The initial pictures Winston chose, the Catherine Wheel and noughts and crosses, showed Winston as stuck in his 'pastimes' and stuck in the 'past (times)'. The final picture he chose, the pack of cards, opened up aspects of his life that troubled him but that he had previously not found words to express. This seems important, despite his scores on specific evaluative measures increasing, and this may reflect him finding a voice and moving forward to voice his concerns.

Furthermore, this evaluation does not have to be potentially influenced by the pre-imposition of medicalised notions of anxiety, depression, phobias, and clinical ranges, thus enabling a more 'phenomenological' approach to evaluation. Importantly, the photographs were used within a psychotherapeutic process and were not introduced as evaluative measures or phototherapeutic techniques.

Using photographs as a potential evaluation of therapeutic change may be a beneficial and complementary, if not alternative, method to evaluation approaches such as the GAD-7, PHQ-9, and CORE-10. Further, such approaches have the advantage of allowing something to emerge that is not predefined by a medical model of diagnosis and treatment, and therefore does not start with a predetermined notion of clinical success. The fact that pathology and diagnosis are not normally a part of school counsellors' daily roles and competencies further supports this method as a possible intervention within schools. However, it could be useful to explore the phototherapeutic interventions used in this study alongside other possible effects and interventions, such as the therapeutic relationship established between the therapist and the clients. In turn, by decreasing future researcher bias, a diverse method of capturing data, such as that from observations, interviews, and school data, could be organised to evaluate the children's progress.

A particularly important area for future research would appear to be how young people are referred for therapy. Often, this would appear to be through the encouragement of others, and sometimes it would appear that the referrer has more difficulty coping with the client's story than the client does. In these settings, there also seems to be much more opportunity for collusion between the counsellor and others employed at the school. It is recommended that phototherapy in schools be carried out by people with, at least, some basic counselling training, both to enable them to help the young person follow their own direction and because those with counselling training have been taught to maintain a greater awareness of personal biases.

Overall conclusion

This chapter has explored both phototherapy and therapeutic photography as research in their own right and the application of current quantitative and qualitative research methods.

With regard to the research case presented, evaluative data measures (see Figure 11.2) of three of the clients (Charlotte, Amanda, and Linda) included a decrease in the PHQ-9 score between pre-and post-evaluation, alongside a decrease in CORE-10 score. Further, both Amanda and Linda scored higher on GAD-7 at pre- than post-therapy evaluation. With regard to Winston, both PHQ-9 and CORE-10 scores increased between pre- and post-therapy. The PHQ-9, CORE-10, GAD-7, and the IAPT Phobia Scale were used as evaluation tools because they are the main culturally accepted approaches to evaluation in the UK. (However, perhaps what could be argued as a better source of approaches for children and adolescents, rather than relying on outcome measure tools that are validated for the adult population, can be found in www.corc.uk.net/media/1950/201404guide_to_using_outcomes_measures_and_feedback_tools-updated.pdf). It was found that they can, however, work against more phenomenological approaches to therapy. For example, the asking of questions can produce an expectation that the therapist is then going to solve the problem, as in, for example, a medical model, which therefore only suits a particular type of therapy. Then again, it was found that having such a framework that starts with asking questions can be a way for both clients and therapists to temporarily reduce the anxiety of 'two frightened people in a room' (Bion 1990: 5).

Again, if the evaluation is done by someone other than a therapist (which can be seen to have a potentially less damaging effect on the therapeutic relationship), there is the further concern as to the client's experience of having to speak, possibly for the first time, with one therapist and then another. Further, all four clients appeared to respond more thoughtfully to the CORE-10 than to the PHQ-9 or GAD-7; perhaps as CORE-10 was the last questionnaire, it was possible that they had gained more practice.

This example is of research into the effectiveness of phototherapy as a method. However, within this, the participants' choices of photograph and the meanings they attach to them perhaps demonstrates even more phototherapy as an important means of research. This potential of the use of photographs as an evaluation of therapeutic change seems particularly worthy of further development and use given that, as mentioned, photography has become so much more a part of everyday life with the advent of smart phones and social media. Thus, using photographs as a potential evaluation method for therapeutic change may be a beneficial and complementary, if not alternative, approach to evaluation methods such as the GAD-7, PHQ-9, and CORE-10.

References

Banks, M. (2001). *Visual Methods in Social Research*. London: Sage.

Barkham, M., Bewick, B., Mullin, T., Gilbody, S., Connell, J., Cahill, J., and Evans, C. (2012). The CORE-10: A short measure of psychological distress for routine use in the psychological therapies. *Counselling and Psychotherapy Research*, 13(1): 1–11.

Bion, W. R. (1990). *Brazilian Lectures*. London: Karnac.

Bleicher, J. (1980). *Contemporary Hermeneutics*. London: Routledge & Kegan Paul.

Christogiorgos, S., Stavrou, E., Widdershoven-Zervaki, M. A., and Tsiantis, J. (2010). Brief psychodynamic psychotherapy in adolescent depression: Two case studies. *Psychoanalytic Psychotherapy*, 24(3): 262–278.

Comfort, C. E. (1985). Published pictures as psychotherapeutic tools. *Arts in Psychotherapy*, 12(4): 245–256.

Freud, S. (1915). Repression. *Standard Edition*, 14: 141–158.

Gadamer, H. (2013). *Truth and Method*. London: Bloomsbury Academic.

Greenwood, D., and Loewenthal, D. (2005). Case study as a means of researching social work and improving practitioner education. *Journal of Social Work Practice*, 19(2): 181–193.

Greenwood, D., and Loewenthal, D. (2007). A case of case study method: The possibility of psychotherapy with a person diagnosed with dementia. In D. Loewenthal (ed.), *Case Studies in Relational Research*, pp. 88–113. Basingstoke: Palgrave Macmillan.

Guy, A., Loewenthal, D., Thomas, R., and Stephenson, S. (2012). Scrutinising NICE: The impact of the national institute for health and clinical excellence guidelines on the provision of counselling and psychotherapy in primary care in the UK. *Psychodynamic Practice*, 18(1).

Halkola, U. (2013). A photograph as a therapeutic experience. In D. Loewenthal (ed.), *Phototherapy and Therapeutic Photography in a Digital Age*. London: Routledge.

Halkola, U., and Koffert, T. (2011). The many stories of being. In U. Halkola, T. Koffert, L. Koulu, M. Krappala, D. Loewenthal, C. Parrella, and P. Pehunen (eds.), *PhotoTherapy-Europe: Learning and Healing with Phototherapy – A Handbook*, pp. 17–24. Turku, Finland: University of Turku: Publications of the Brahea Centre for Training and Development.

Heidegger, M. (1962). *Being and Time*. Oxford: Blackwell Publishing.

Higher Education Funding Council for England. (2014). *Research Excellence Framework 2014: The Results: Part 3, Section 2, Para 115*. www.ref.ac.uk/2014/media/ref/content/pub/REF%2001%202014%20-%20full%20document.pdf.

Horn, H., Geiser-Elze, A., Reck, C., Hartmann, M., Stefini, A., Victor, D., and Kronmuller, T. (2005). Zur wirksamheit psychodynamischer kurzzeit-psychotherapie bei kindern und jugendlichen mit depressionen [Efficacy of psychodynamic short-term psychotherapy for children and adolescents with depression]. *Praxis Der Kinderpsychologie Und Kinderpsychiatrie*, 54: 578–597.

Krauss, D., and Fryrear, J. (1983). *Phototherapy in Mental Health*. Springfield, IL: Charles C. Thomas Pub Ltd.

Lees, J., and Freshwater, D. (2008). *Practitioner-Based Research: Power, Discourse, and Transformation*. London: Karnac Books.

Loewenthal, D. (2007). *Case Studies in Relational Research*. Basingstoke: Palgrave Macmillan.

Loewenthal, D. (2009). Can photographs help one find one's voice? The use of photographs in the psychological therapies [Editorial]. *European Journal of Psychotherapy and Counseling*, 11(1): 1–6.

Loewenthal, D. (2010). Picture book. *Every Child Journal*, 1(3): 10–12.

Loewenthal, D. (2011). Researching phototherapy and therapeutic photography. In U. Halkola, T. Koffert, M. Krappola, D. Loewenthal, C. Parrella, and P. Pehunen (eds.), *Phototherapy-Europe: Learning and Healing with Phototherapy – A Handbook*, pp. 17–24. Turku, Finland: University of Turku: Publications of the Brahea Centre for Training and Development.

Loewenthal, D. (2013). *Phototherapy and Therapeutic Photography in a Digital Age*. Hove: Routledge.

Loewenthal, D. (2016). Therapy as cultural, politically influenced practice. In J. Lees (ed.), *The Future of Psychological Therapy: Managed Care, Practitioner Research and Clinical Innovation*, pp. 11–25. London: Routledge.

Loewenthal, D., and Winter, D. (eds.). (2007). *What Is Psychotherapeutic Research?* London: Karnac Books.

Mannay, D. (2010). Making the familiar strange: Can visual research methods render the familiar setting more perceptible? *Qualitative Research*, 10(1): 91–111.

Martin, R., and Spence, J. (1987). New portraits for old: The use of the camera in therapy. In R. Betterton (ed.), *Looking on: Images of Femininity in the Visual Arts and Media*, pp. 267–279. London: Pandora.

Martin, R., and Spence, J. (1988). Phototherapy: Psychic realism as a healing art? *Ten*, 8(30): 2–10.

Muratori, F., Picchi, L., Casetta, C., Tancredi, R., Milone, A., and Patarnello, M. G. (2002). Efficacy of brief dynamic psychotherapy for children with emotional disorders. *Psychotherapy and Psychosomatics*, 71: 28–38. https://doi.org/10.1159/000049341.

Pauwels, L. (2011). An integrated conceptual framework for visual social research. In E. Margolis and L. Pauwels (eds.), *The Sage Handbook of Visual Research Methods*, 1st edition, pp. 3–23. London: Sage.

Phillips, D. (1986). Photography's use as a metaphor of self with stabilized schizophrenic patients. *Arts in Psychotherapy*, 13(1): 9–16. https://doi.org/10.1016/0197-4556(86)90004-3.

Princeton Wordnet Web. (2006). *Frascati Definition*. University of Oxford. http://wordnet. princeton.edu/perl/webwn?s=word-you-want (Accessed April 2011).

Prosser, J. (2006). The darker side of visual research. In P. Hamilton (ed.), *Visual Research Methods*. London: Sage.

RAE. (2008). *Research Assessment Exercise*. www.rae.ac.uk (Accessed April 2011).

Spence, J. (1986). *Putting Myself in the Picture: A Political, Personal and Photographic Autobiography*. London: Camden Press.

Sponseller, D. B. (1979). *Photographic Feedback Effects on Preschool Exceptional Children's Self-Concept and Social Competence*. Paper presented at the 57th Annual International Convention of the Council for Exceptional Children, Dallas, TX, April.

Walker, J. (1986). The use of ambiguous artistic images for enhancing self-awareness in psychotherapy. *Arts in Psychotherapy*, 13(3): 241–248. https://doi.org/10.1016/0197-4556 (86)90050-X.

Weiser, J. (1999). *Phototherapy Techniques: Exploring the Secrets of Personal Snapshots and Family Albums*, 2nd edition. Vancouver: Phototherapy Centre.

Weiser, J. (2000). Phototherapy's message for art therapies in the new millennium. *Journal of the American Art Therapy Association*, 17(3): 160–162. www.phototherapy-centre.com/articles/2000_PhTmillenm.pdf.

Weiser, J. (2001). PhotoTherapy techniques: Using clients' personal snapshots and family photos as counselling and therapy tools. *Afterimage: The Journal of Media Arts and Cultural Criticism*, 29(3): 10–15.

Weiser, J. (2002). Phototherapy techniques: Exploring the secrets of personal snapshots and family albums. *Child and Family*, 16–25, Spring–Summer. www.phototherapy-centre.com/Weiser_BCPA_08.pdf.

Weiser, J. (2004). Phototherapy techniques in counselling and therapy – using ordinary snapshots and photo-interactions to help clients heal their lives. *The Canadian Art Therapy Association Journal*, 17(2): 23–53.

Yin, R. (1984). *Case Study Research: Design and Methods*, 1st edition. Beverly Hills, CA: Sage.

Yin, R. (2014). *Case Study Research Design and Methods*, 5th edition. Thousand Oaks, CA: Sage.

12 Bringing it all together

Training yourself and others as phototherapists and therapeutic photographers and facilitating workshops

Summary

There are four aims of this final chapter. The first is to consider the training of phototherapy and therapeutic photography practitioners. Next, training plans are provided for integration into existing training programmes for counsellors, psychotherapists, psychologists, arts and play therapists. Then, a five-day stand-alone programme (based on a number of such programmes provided for related professions in various European countries) is described. A case study of such a five-day programme is detailed. The fourth aim is to provide some concluding thoughts on current and future phototherapy and therapeutic photography practices.

The case study given describes a phototherapy and therapeutic photography workshop for a group of young LGBT+ participants (illustrated in Photo 12.1) to facilitate their emotional learning. This is also used to show how phototherapy and therapeutic photography can be carried out in group as well as in one-on-one settings.

The training and workshop descriptions also provide the opportunity for 'bringing it all together'. Hence, this chapter ends with 'Conclusions' and 'The future', followed by a final assignment as you embark on your own continuous phototherapy and therapeutic photography professional development.

Key learning points

1. The important distinction between phototherapy and therapeutic photography is made. While in the former case, it is it the therapist who engages in phototherapy, in the latter it can also be the activist client or adult educator who engages in the process of therapeutic photography.
2. Research shows that therapeutic use of photographs significantly helps the majority of clients.
3. In rare cases, the therapeutic use of photographs can be too much too soon, and the therapist needs to then know how to respond.
4. It is assumed we can never be absolutely sure if we are saying something, or not saying something, for ourselves or our client. Personal therapy and supervision are regarded as essential prerequisites for carrying out phototherapy and are recommended for therapeutic photography.

DOI: 10.4324/9781003240914-13

Photo 12.1 Phototherapy and Therapeutic workshop for young LGBT+ people

5. There is a difficult question as to when someone is ready to use photographs therapeutically on others. There are many psychological therapists and allied professionals who do not receive personal therapy. There are also many areas where there is a shortage of psychological therapists, but there are others with considerable experience of facilitating others.
6. Psychological therapists and others in the helping professions can learn how to therapeutically use photographs by developing their own learning plan and having appropriate supervision.
7. As with individual and group therapy, clients can benefit from receiving phototherapy and therapeutic photography either one-on-one or in a group/workshop.
8. It is considered important that phototherapists and therapeutic photographers have their own support network, both for themselves as people and to have a good basis for helping others.
9. The activist client should also have their own support network and be prepared to have external supervision and further personal therapy should the need arise.
10. Attention needs to be given to minimise clients/activist clients getting stuck in premature closure whereby photography initially moves them on, only for the client to get stuck in a new place.
11. The therapeutic use of photographs can be beneficially employed within the various psychological therapies and in other helping professions.
12. Not only is a picture worth a thousand words but words may not come into being without a picture!

Exercise

Develop your abilities further by following one of the lessons plans provided here, either as a facilitator or activist client. Rate your facilitation of others or yourself on the evaluation scales provided.

Training phototherapists and therapeutic photographers

The following is the outline of my five-day phototherapy training programme:

Facilitating emotional learning through the use of photographs

(Day one)

• Introductions and overview of the programme
• History and theories of phototherapy and therapeutic photography
• What are we being sensitive to and how?
• Introduction to empathy, unconditional positive regard, and congruence
• The use of Photocards in psychological therapy, education, and other professions

Facilitating emotional learning through the use of photographs

(Day two)

• Categories of interventions and working with photographs important to participants

Facilitating emotional learning through the use of photographs

(Day three)

• Further exercises in facilitating emotional learning
• The use of Photocards in story books and digital story telling

Facilitating emotional learning through the use of photographs

(Day four)

• Further exercises in facilitating emotional learning
• Employability: PhotoVoice/force field analysis

Facilitating emotional learning through the use of photographs

(Day five)

• Further exercises in facilitating emotional learning
• Portraiture and review

There now follows a number of lesson guides for which I gratefully acknowledge the assistance of my colleagues (and particularly Monica Accordini from the Catholic University of the Sacred Heart, Milan, Italy) in the Grundtvig Lifelong Learning Programme (https://artescommunity.eu/photherapyeurope-in-prisons/).

Such lesson guides are for the therapist who engages in phototherapy, the activist client, or the adult educator who engages in the process of therapeutic photographer and can be modified according to need to train individuals interested in working in the four approaches to phototherapy and therapeutic photography described in previous chapters. Each of the following lesson plans provides a number of activities for the training session. Facilitators are encouraged to complement these activities with other activities so that trainees will understand the theory in which therapy and phototherapy are embedded. Facilitators are encouraged to develop handouts and other supporting material that supplement the main ideas of these lesson plans.

The lesson guides are:

1. Phototherapy (Figure 12.1)
2. Listening and reflecting (Figure 12.2)
3. The use of photographs for phototherapy (Figure 12.3)
4. The development of Photobooks (Figure 12.4)
5. The use of photography for action (Figure 12.5)

Also, lesson plans are not provided here for all the approaches in this handbook, but facilitators can devise lesson plans for them on the basis of the formats already used.

All trainers are strongly recommended to complete a group contract *before* commencing any training programme with participant learners. This can include a discussion on confidentiality and all learner participants to be made aware that they should practise self-care during sessions by not revealing information that might make them feel too vulnerable during the training. Similarly, any references to clients/patients and workplaces should be made without identifying information or material.

There then follow two further figures. The first is a handout entitled 'Review of the phototherapy interview' (Figure 12.6). This is written for the client to review the phototherapist but is also recommended as a useful instrument for the phototherapist/therapeutic photographer to review their own experience of the sessions.

The final figure in this section is an evaluation template that can be used either for a particular session/day and/or the entire workshop. Again, it is recommended that the trainer/facilitator also fill in the template. However, with regard to evaluation, it is very strongly recommended that workshop participants at least also choose a Photocard from a set to describe to the group their experience of the session/day/course.

These are then followed by some additional points with regard to ethics and confidentiality which are specific to such training and have not been covered to the same extent in previous chapters.

My main experience of using lesson plans, such as the following, is for a lesson plan day to be held once a week for five weeks. Though, in practice, they can be used in various formats.

Training session plan 1: Phototherapy

Time	Aims and objectives	Outcomes expected for learners	Resources	Activities
1 hr.	Preparing to work in the particular environment/context	To explore how working with this group may differ from working with other groups.	Flip charts and pens.	In groups, participants write how they think working with their client group may differ from working with other groups. Present to the whole group and discuss. Facilitators should discuss and challenge group ideas, particularly prejudice, judgements, etc., and then explore and discuss specific working practices in their contexts.
30 min.	Therapy	Learners will be provided with a short introduction to the various models of therapy available.		Introduction to psychotherapy
1 hr.	Confidentiality in reference to practice	Learners will be aware of confidentiality in reference to phototherapy	Sample of documentation: Confidentiality statement	Introduction to confidentiality
1 hr.	Breaching confidentiality	Learners will know when it may be necessary to breach confidentiality	Role play material	Confidentiality breaches – examples of when this happens. Times when confidentiality may be broken. Role play: Scenarios are created. and the learners have to discuss – and decide – if confidentiality at this point is to be broken.
1 hr.	Risk	Learners will have basic understanding of risk assessment skills		Introduction to risk and risk assessment.
30 min.	Evaluation/feedback	Learners are provided with space to give feedback	Session evaluation form (Figure 12.7).	Evaluation of session. Identification of positives of the session, what could have been done better and suggestions of how the same session can be improved for the future.

Figure 12.1 Training session plan 1: Phototherapy

Training session plan 2: Listening and reflecting

Time	Aims and objectives	Outcomes expected for learners	Resources	Activities
1 hr. 30 min.	Listening skills	To explore issues and problems in listening and responding	Photocards	In pairs, each learner selects a card which they feel best describes how they are feeling now. Each talks for five minutes about themselves in relation to the card. Each learner then introduces their partner to the whole group in terms of how their partner feels. Trainer then explores where this was difficult, where someone forgets, etc.
1 hr.	Listening and responding	To address potential problems with listening and responding. Assess current skills.		Explore the last exercise, discuss problems in listening/responding, and learn how to improve listening skills
1 hr.	Paraphrasing and summarising skills	Improve on current listening skills		Introduce paraphrasing as a listening skill. In pairs, have learners repeat the introductory exercise using paraphrasing. Feedback to whole group.
30 min	Reflecting content and underlying feelings	Bringing together listening, responding, and interpretation		In pairs, explore the underlying content within the introductory exercise. Discuss how interpretations vary, meanings change and feedback to group. Pay particular attention to the differences in interpretation for the same cards – discuss as a group.
1 hr.	Roger's Core Conditions	Learning provided with basic therapeutic theory and skills		Introduce Roger's Core Conditions. Explain person-centred approach. Explore core conditions and their uses.
30 min.	Review of skills.	Learners provided with space to practise new skills	Photocards	The group swaps partners, chooses news card to reflect how they are feeling, and tells their partners. The partners use the skills taught in the session and then introduce new partners to the group. Whole group discussion on how the skills may have improved listening, remembering, and responding.
30 min.	Evaluation and feedback	Learners are provided with space to give their feedback, monitor skills learnt, and improve future training.	Session evaluation form (Figure 12.7).	Evaluation of the session. Identification of positives of the session, what could have been done better, and suggestions of how the same session can be improved for the future.

Figure 12.2 Training session plan 2: Listening and responding

Training session plan 3: The use of Photocards for phototherapy

Time	Aims and objectives	Outcomes expected for learners	Resources	Activities
1 hr.	To familiarise learners with materials.	Familiarity with Photocards Familiarity with materials used in phototherapy	Photocards Photocards	Continuation on the use of Photocards Explore cards in groups
2 hr.	To practise skills from the earlier session with the Photocard materials.	To help learners reflect on each role and explore person-centred approaches with the use of Photocards To explore empathic interpretation skills.	Photocards Feedback sheets for observers (Figure 12.6)	Group exercise: In groups of three, one participant is the client, the other the therapist, and the third the observer. The client chooses a card, and the therapist explores (using the core conditions and skills learnt in session plan 2) and helps to interpret and explore with client. The observer makes notes for feedback. Each group has 15 minutes in each role.
1 hr.	To understand the practice and process of using Photocards	To help learners understand how to use Photocards as well as how to record and reflect on sessions.	Handout: Case example (see Chapter 2)	Each individual trainee reads the handout. The handout is discussed in pairs. The main conclusions are discussed in class.
30 min.	Evaluation and feedback	Learners provided with space to give their feedback	Session evaluation form (Figure 12.7).	Evaluation of session. Identification of positives of the session, what could have been done better, and suggestions of how the same session can be improved for the future.

Figure 12.3 Training session plan 3: The use of Photocards for phototherapy

Training session plan 4: The development of Photobooks

Time	Aims and objectives	Outcomes expected for learners	Resources	Activities
1 hr.	Familiarise participants with materials	Familiarise with Photobook development and concept	Photobook	Group introduction to Photobooks. Study sample and understand concept behind it
2 hr.	To use materials in practice.	Experience in practice and to receive feedback on skills.	Photobook observation sheets (see Assignment Exercise, Chapter 4)	In groups of three, each participant is either the client, therapist, or observer. Each has opportunity to develop their own Photobook, explore it, facilitate another, and to observe.
1 hr.	Practise with skills and materials.	To practise with materials, reflect on their own practice, and use skills.	Handout: Photo emotional writing: A case study around the Photobook approach (see case study Chapter 4)	Groups repeat the previous exercise, using all skills learnt in the programme.
30 min.	Evaluation and feedback	Learners are provided with space to give their feedback.	Session evaluation form (see Figure 12.7)	Evaluation of session. Identification of positives of the session, what could have been done better, and suggestions on how the same session can be improved for the future.

Figure 12.4 Training session plan 4: The development of Photobooks

Training session plan 5: The use of photography for action (for example, rehabilitation and employability)

Time	Aims and objectives	Outcomes expected for learners	Resources	Activities
30 min.	Familiarise participants with concepts.	Basic understanding.	Photocards Flip charts	Introduction to course basics.
2 hr.	Basic introduction to using materials for employability.	Basic introduction to aims of using phototherapy for employability.	Handout (see Chapter 8)	Introduction to phototherapy for employability
	To provide a basic introduction to force field analysis.	Facilitate skills in force field analysis.		Introduction to force field analysis.
1 hr.	To bring together skills, materials, and force field analysis	Improve skills and expand to using for rehabilitation and employability	Photocards (Observation sheets can also be devised)	Group work using materials and force field analysis. Therapist, client, observer.
1 hr.	Employability through Photocards in practice.	Understand how to employ the concept to employability.		To discuss the reflective writing in the handout.
30 min.	Evaluation and feedback	Learners are provided with space to give feedback.	Session evaluation form (Figure 12.7)	Evaluation of session. Identification of positives of the session, what could have been done better, and suggestions on how the same session can be improved for the future.

Figure 12.5 Training session plan 5: The use of photography for action

Handout: Review of the phototherapy interview

Name of Trainee Phototherapist: _____

Date: _____

Circle the number which you feel best expresses the approach of the phototherapy/
  therapeutic photography facilitator.

Key:	1 Very good 2 Good	3 Average	4 Fair		5 Poor	
	1	**2**	**3**	**4**	**5**	
Ability to listen and reflect back what the client says						
Ability to reflect back what the client is feeling						
Ability to occasionally reflect back what the client is making the facilitator feel						
Ability to follow the clients lead						
Ability to accept and not judge the client						
Ability to enable appropriate silences						
Ability to enable the client to follow their own path						
Ability to appropriately bracket where the client's story reminds the facilitator of their story						
What would you regard as the facilitator's strengths of this session?						
Which skills do you consider the facilitator needs help in improving?						

Figure 12.6 Handout: Review of the phototherapy interview

Handout: Session/day/workshop evaluation form

Please answer the following questions:

1. Please indicate on the following regarding your experience of this session/day/workshop?
Very good   Good   Average   Poor   Very Poor
2. Please describe further your response to question 1.
3. What do you regard as particularly helpful in what you have been presented with?

What suggestions have you for what could be improved in future provision of a similar training event?

Figure 12.7 Session evaluation form

Ethical requirements

1. Facilitators need to know the existing ethical systems and processes in place within the country/professional body/organisation.
2. Limits to disclosure are to be managed by the facilitator, adhering to the policy of the relevant therapeutic service (for example, that any risk of serious harm to self or others would be reported).
3. Participation in any phototherapy or therapeutic photography as clients or trainees must be strictly voluntary and there must be no impact on any potential participant who decides not to volunteer. Facilitators will conform to locally applicable health and safety requirements.
4. Individual and group therapeutic and training sessions must be confidential.

Confidentiality and risk assessment

Each country/professional body/organisation may have its own confidentiality contract clauses and risk assessment procedures. These should be provided to all trainees in the first training session.

A confidentiality statement example

Confidentiality statements and their clauses may vary in different environments and countries and in respect to different populations. The statement provided here (Figure 12.8) is only given as an example. Before any trainees work with clients, they should ensure that the client is aware of confidentiality boundaries and specific times that confidentiality may have to be broken. Trainees should also be made aware of possible breaches of client confidentiality (see more on this in the following example).

Example of a confidentiality statement:

During our phototherapy/therapeutic photography sessions, I will respect your confidentiality. This means that during our sessions, what you tell me will remain confidential between us. However, there are some specific times when you may tell me something and I will be obliged to break my confidentiality with you and report some of what you have told me in those sessions.
  Times I may have to break confidentiality would be:

- *If you reveal that you may harm yourself.*
- *If you reveal that you may harm another person.*
- *If you reveal any possible future or past risk to a minor.*

Figure 12.8 Example of a confidentiality statement

Explaining confidentiality statements and clauses to vulnerable people

Some clients we work with may be particularly vulnerable to misunderstanding confidentiality statements and agreements. For this reason, it is imperative that all trainees are aware of those who may require extra guidance with regard to confidentiality during phototherapy sessions. Some examples of these are those with:

- Learning disabilities
- Psychiatric diagnoses
- Cognitive and memory deficits
- High-risk presentations (for example those who may self-harm or are suicidal)

In these cases, trainees may be advised to:

- Repeat the confidentiality statement at the beginning of each session
- Provide examples of times when confidentiality may have to be broken
- Discuss why confidentiality may be broken in more depth
- Ask the client to demonstrate their understanding by explaining back to you the confidentiality agreement and clauses

Case: A phototherapy and therapeutic photography workshop for young LGBT+ people

As discussed in Chapter 1, our clients, particularly younger ones, are very familiar with communicating with photographs given the advent of Facebook, WhatsApp, Snapchat, Instagram, etc. I now will bring together some of the main approaches detailed in this handbook by describing a workshop I ran for young LGBT+ participants. In so doing, it is hoped that this chapter section will not only be of help to those wanting to run workshops but for psychological therapists who wish to explore how they can effectively integrate the use of photographs into their practices. The workshop participants had come together, as one of the participants said, with general agreement, 'to understand myself and people around me'.

Five main approaches as outlined in Chapter 1 of this book (Loewenthal 2013a, 2018) were examined that might more often be singularly used within a traditional one to one therapy session rather than as here employed together over 5 weekly workshop sessions with a group. The five approaches are:

1. As in Chapter 2: The therapeutic use of photographs/Photocards (most often called 'phototherapy')
2. As in Chapter 3: The taking of therapeutic photographs (most often called 'therapeutic photography')
3. As in Chapter 4: The therapeutic creation of Photobooks
4. As in Chapter 8: The development of action plans through photography
5. As in Chapter 9: The therapeutic use of portraiture (including 'selfies').

First regarding the 'therapeutic use of photographs/Photocards' (most often called 'phototherapy' – see Chapter 2 and, for example, Weiser 1993 [1999], Loewenthal 2013b, and Craig 2009). As mentioned in Chapter 2, Photocards, which usually can comprise up to fifty or sixty postcard-sized photographs, are used particularly at the start of therapy. Placing the cards on a table or floor, sometimes with the client's help, can also be a useful icebreaker. The client is then asked to choose a photograph that calls to them, followed by the question, 'Why did you choose that photo?'.

In my first meeting with this LGBT+ group, Frankie (all names have been changed) chose a photograph of the sea and sky, saying it reminded her how she once wanted to be a marine biologist and she had forgotten about what she really wanted to be until she saw the photograph. After we explored this with her, another participant, Fay, chose a photograph of some footprints in the sand, and she spoke of the place she once lived where she could look out to sea 'with the whole world behind me'. Hannah couldn't make up her mind which of two photographs to choose, and this later seemed an important pattern for her. Hannah did eventually choose one of some stairs going up, which she said was 'scary'. Next, Dom chose one of a bench, saying, 'It looked so sad'. We continued for each group member, reflecting back and opening up space until it was felt time to move to the next person.

The idea is that these clients are quickly bringing to awareness what is on their minds, projecting what has been repressed. This enables the therapist to work more quickly within their therapeutic modality. The client can be asked to choose a photograph whenever the therapist considers it helpful. The photos themselves do not have a universal meaning, rather the meaning is always particular to the client at that moment.

Soon after starting, a member of the group raised a question as to how they might respond to what others said. I wondered with them how we might do this in ways that would be particularly useful to others as well. This also led to personal explorations of how it is all too easy not to meet others and be lonely in a city.

Later, we chose Photocards in a way that another facilitator had suggested to me. The first Photocard was to represent *who I am*.

Peter, for example, chose an apple which was unusual as it had an extra piece growing on it. Peter said he was different in a similar way.

After going around the group exploring how each member came to make their choice, group members were then asked to choose a photograph to represent *who I used to be*.

The third photograph participants were asked to choose was *who others or significant others think I am*. The fourth prompt was to choose a photograph that came to mind when asked *what do I want to be?*. The group also came up with their own questions, including choosing photographs of *something I don't like*, and then *something I do like*.

Regarding the taking of therapeutic photographs (most often called 'therapeutic photography' – see Chapter 3 and, for example, Spence 1986, Martin 2013, Gibson 2018, and Loewenthal 2013b).

Therapeutic photography involves taking photographs to explore thoughts and feelings regarding, for example, a bereavement, and traditionally has not always involved a psychological therapist. With this particular group, it was not set as 'homework' (photographic tasks participants carried out between our weekly meetings) but instead a variation was used as described when taking selfies.

Regarding 'the therapeutic creation of Photobooks' (see Chapter 4 and Loewenthal 2015a)– at the start of our second meeting, I introduced the participants to creating Photobooks. This was something I had devised when working with prisoners (Chapter 4 and Loewenthal 2015a) and had proved very popular with clients (Loewenthal 2015b) and in my training of art psychotherapists. Again, whilst the books themselves appear a useful way of working through emotional constructions, much can also arise in facilitating the process. For example, a participant who wanted to do a book for her sister when asked to choose a photograph of good memories responded very emotionally saying, 'But I do not have any good memories of my sister!', which she was then able to explore.

Regarding 'the therapeutic use of portraiture including "selfies"' (see Chapter 9 and Nunez 2009) – in week three, we also took selfies on our mobiles. This led to various explorations with each member of the group, starting with their responses to their selfie:

For example, Peter said, 'I like the fact I look quite good. I usually probably look bad'.

Mo said, 'My hair looks fine, but my face looks fat. I look like a chilled person. I can look like a groupie person. I like my make-up. I put effort into my appearance'.

Hessa stated, '50000 lilies. I like, I look innocent. I look like a cute Arabian girl. One eye is bigger than the other. I want to be perfection'.

Hannah said, 'I'm quite shy at first; I like the symmetry about myself, it doesn't show my full potential'.

Dom stated, 'I like to represent humour and not be too serious. I hate my shiny head and receding hair line – it shows my age and I'm old, I don't like the shapes of my eyes'.

One recurring question for the group was the extent to which appearances reflect personality.

Regarding 'The development of action plans through photography' (see Chapter 8 and Loewenthal 2015a) – for our week 4 meeting, the Photocards were used in order for participants to develop action plans for something they wanted to achieve. Once having identified this aim, it was represented by drawing a straight horizontal line. Participants then chose a Photocard that represented the greatest external force stopping them achieving this, and this was drawn upwards as a vertical line to the horizontal line, with a length equivalent to the strength of the force. Two more vertical lines were then drawn, one going downwards and representing the greatest force within the individual that is working against the potential achievements, and the other force coming from below representing the force within the individual that is most helpful. A decision was then made as to where an individual could best put her or his energy in order to reduce any force against and increase any force for. (In one-on-one sessions, where there is more time, several forces for and against can be examined.) Also, it would be possible for participants to clarify the forces for and against by taking photographs that represent them.

Using photographs to evaluate the therapeutic use of photographs

Membership of this group varied considerably from week to week, making such measures as the GAD-7 and PQH-9 difficult to administer and the results inconclusive. Such methods can also appear to be an external imposition on what evolves. What does more easily fit in with the therapeutic and learning process is to ask clients to choose a photo that calls to them at the beginning and end of therapy, or in the case of a course, a photo that represents their experience on the course. Here are some of the comments in the latter case:

Ayesha, on choosing a picture of what she saw as a forest (Photo 7.1d), reported, 'I picked it because I feel very planted like a seed – I feel like I'm going through all my emotions. I've now got in my head what I feel and what I want to feel through the photos'.

Sandra, on choosing a photo of a blue sky with clouds (Photo 7.2b), said, 'It looks like a metaphor for life. The holes are like an experience – a good experience – a unique experience – I've never done it before – it's added to my life'.

Conclusions

Overall, in my experience, most of those whom I have worked with using these approaches in such contexts as schools, prisons, and management development, often on a one-on-one basis, find photographs very helpful. It seems to help the therapist help the client quicker. In fact, a study of the use of Talking Picture Cards in European prisons found that 92 percent of inmates found the use of Photocards 'very helpful' or 'helpful' (Loewenthal 2015b). This research, where I was the principal investigator, found the main themes emerging regarding participants' experiences of working with Photocards were that it:

- Facilitates emotional expression and sharing
- Unlocks memories and reconnects with life outside
- Fosters insight, reflection, and self-growth
- Breaks the monotony
- Aids in emotional learning overall

Furthermore, an analysis of the psychological therapist's/facilitator's perspectives suggested that the use of Photocards:

- Gives clients a voice
- Provides a safe and collaborative frame, a therapeutic relationship
- Provides a useful icebreaker, helpful for overcoming anxieties of both the client and the psychotherapist/facilitator

Overall, Photocards were considered useful, as their projective nature can help facilitate a strong need for expression, particularly in contexts where there are limited opportunities and trust is fragile. Nevertheless, more research is required (both quantitative and qualitative) that explores the experience of clients who have made use of photographs in their therapy to evaluate further the claim that photographs can effectively speed up access to, and the working through of, repressed thoughts and feelings.

I do, though, think there are a few clients for whom the use of photography makes relatively little difference, and very occasionally, their use is too much too soon. This, for example, did happen when there was a photograph of some graffiti on a wall and the client had been molested against such a wall on her way to school. In this case, I put the photographs away and we successfully continued the session without them.

Photocard sets can be purchased, or a set of mine can be downloaded for free from my 52 Talking Pictures (located at www.delloewenthal.com/phototherapy-and-therapeutic-photography.html). If you do wish to make your own, I recommend having ordinary shots on which the client can project. (It is not necessary, and can sometimes be a distraction, to have aesthetically pleasing photographs. Furthermore, I don't recommend dramatic or violent images – our clients usually have more than enough of those in their lives!)

Importantly, as I have tried to stress throughout this book, there is a tendency to regard therapeutic photography as not requiring a trained counsellor or psychotherapist and then calling any therapeutic use of photographs 'therapeutic photography'. Nearly anyone can ask another to choose a photograph that calls to them, but it is strongly recommended that this is best done within the practice of a trained psychological therapist who has had a significant period of their own personal therapy. It may seem relatively easy to start to instruct the client as to what to do, but far more difficult to continue with interventions that are therapeutically appropriate.

Therapist/facilitator styles

In contrast to the earlier use of Talking Picture Cards in brief counselling/psychotherapy, other approaches require the facilitator to also be more directional. The use of Talking Picture Books appeared to the facilitator to raise the strongest positive feelings within prison inmates, even though, on some level, many perhaps knew that in reality it wasn't going to work out with their child and their child's mother how they had dreamt. There is also the question of how much the therapist should collude with the imaginary. However, as can hopefully be seen in the case study presented of Demario in Chapter 4, the therapeutic relationship becomes important even though one might start with such a structure. This move to more authoritative as well as facilitative interventions (Heron 1986) is also true for the approach of photo-assisted employability/rehabilitation. Asking an inmate to list internal and external helps and hindrances and explore them either by taking photographs (as reported in Chapter 8) or using the Photocards is directional, as is the subsequent use of force field analysis in order to determine the priority action to be taken.

However, facilitating people in taking photographs or choosing Photocards needs to be non-directional. Once again, the relationship established appears crucial.

As in this book's case studies, all approaches appear to provide significant contributions to clients' emotional learning. The use of Photocards appears, in contrast to the facilitator's experience in providing brief therapy without photographs, to enable clients to speak more quickly of what was on their mind (Loewenthal 2013a). It appears particularly helpful to those who might usually have difficulty in expressing their concerns because of what photographs are able to help them elicit, and because clients are able to be actively involved in the process. As suggested by Bucci (1999) and Saita et al. (2014), humans do not function using only a verbal code; the use of photos facilitates more complex linking processes between the non-verbal and verbal systems that could not be spontaneously engaged by the person, for example Chapter 5. The main disadvantage of using Photocards in brief counselling and psychotherapy was that occasionally a client expresses too much too soon. Furthermore, the facilitator needs to be an experienced practitioner and, for example, one who can stay working with despair (Gee and Loewenthal 2013).

The future

Such approaches that allow the photograph for the disembodied client to come to mind have the advantage of allowing something to emerge which is not pre-defined. This is in contrast, for example, to a medicalised model of diagnosis and treatment, and hence starting without a pre-determined notion of clinical success. This change in language through digital photography changes culturally what, and how, we experience, not only in terms of being able to look back on such websites as Facebook as to what photos we and others posted of ourselves, but the very nature of our experiences. Perhaps this change in our way of perceiving and thinking will be even greater than when photography, at the start of the 20th century, changed the perception and thinking of so many people, including Sigmund Freud (Bergstein 2010). Importantly, the research is continuing (see for example Ingham et al., 2023).

We might therefore expect to see in our 21st century both the increasing use of photographs in such psychological therapies as counselling and psychotherapy, as well as arts therapies using photographs more creatively rather than just recording various stages of development in the non-photographic artwork (Kopytin 2013).

Photographs are already increasingly used in education and, particularly, as mentioned, in reminiscence therapy with older people (Craig 2014) and those with Alzheimer disease (Krauss 2009). It is also expected that there will be further growth of new forms of therapy using photography where the traditional position taken up by therapists becomes fundamentally different, as in, for example, working alongside each other with a computer. It is further expected there will be rapid developments in the therapeutic use of video (See Cohen 2023; Cohen et al. 2016). Already, artificial intelligence is offering possibilities of turning a client's words into unique pictures (see for example www.midjourney.com/home/). Whilst this is a reverse process to phototherapy's evolving words from a photograph, such AI images open up opportunities to explore the extent to which they have therapeutic potential.

It is also predicted that there will be a growing use of photographs in organisational and individual development, including management development as, for example, described in Chapter 7. The possibilities are endless, but the idea that a digital photograph can describe what is otherwise difficult to put into words remains pertinent.

We might also expect that there will be a growing use of group phototherapy and community phototherapy (see Parella and Loewenthal 2013), where an issue can be worked through and/or brought to the attention of the wider community. A meta-analysis of the effectiveness of creative arts therapies (Stamp et al. 2009) suggests that what is therapeutically important is for clients to carry out a creative act (see Simmons 2013) and share it in a group. Digital images lend themselves particularly well to this, and it is predicted that this will be a popular, cost effective, therapeutic development.

Overall, it is expected that digital photographs will be used more extensively, not only in terms of for example digital storytelling, which is becoming available to school children, but also in a wide range of professional practices and cultural activities, including developments in social media. This will lead to new theories that will need to be increasingly researched and will lead in and of themselves to new research methodologies using digital photography.

What is clear is that the therapeutic power of the photograph to evoke past emotions will continue and be creatively and digitally available on an unprecedented scale. It is also expected that the therapeutic use of photographs will increasingly be used in programmes for psychological therapy, both for trainees and existing practitioners, helping them to get up to date with what their prospective clients are often already familiar.

It would seem the advantages of these approaches are that they enable participants to put into words thoughts and feelings that previously were repressed that either cannot be accessed or take far longer through conventional talking therapies. The main limitations or pitfalls are that, without a trained therapist, participants can open up something but get stuck, not being able to work it through. A particular problem here, to repeat just once more (!) is where those not trained in therapeutic approaches call any method using photographs 'therapeutic photography' with the false argument that this could then be facilitated by anyone. (The frequent usage of 'phototherapy' to include 'therapeutic photography' can further complicate understanding the differences.) Thus, it has been strongly recommended that practitioners first have a recognised therapeutic interpersonal training. This is not usually the case with the training of psychiatrists, clinical psychologists, and behavioural and systemic psychotherapists as well as group psychotherapists (though a few may have had additional training). Otherwise, there is an increasing danger that some will become practitioners by calling what they are doing therapeutic photography to the potential detriment of their clients.

It is hoped that this book will provide a guide for those in various professions to develop their practices by therapeutically using photography. It would appear not only that the therapeutic, digital use of photographs may need to consider other psychotherapeutic research being conducted more generally in the psychological therapies but also that photography can provide a new form of research as a cultural practice, for example by exploring the client's associations with the pre- and post-therapy photographs chosen as a means of evaluation (Chapter 11).

To conclude, there is a growing acknowledgment that phototherapy and therapeutic photography provide an important therapeutic means to enable emotional learning. It is very much hoped that this handbook will enhance emotional learning in clients and activist clients and its facilitation by various professions through the various phototherapy and therapeutic photography approaches herein described.

Final, but not final, assignment: My life in 10 pictures

Now that you are well underway to developing your phototherapy and therapeutic photography abilities, consider up to 10 photos that you think best portray your life. For each photo, write at least a couple sentences as to why you chose that photo. You may already have the photos, but they could include ones you take now or ones taken by others describing your key moments/experiences – you might even consider re-enactment phototherapy (Chapter 5).

Next, do consider and perhaps write down what photos you might change according to with whom you might show '*your life in 10 pictures*'.

All the best for your development through the therapeutic use of photographs!

References

Bergstein, M. (2010). *Mirrors of Memory: Freud, Photography and the History of Art*. London: Cornell University Press.

Bucci, W. (1999). The multiple code theory and the 'third ear'; the role of theory and research in clinical practice. *Psichiatria e Psicoterapia Analitica*, 18: 299–310.

Cohen, J. (ed.). (2023). *Film/Video-Based Therapy and Trauma: Research and Practice*. Abingdon: Routledge.

Cohen, J., Johnson, J., and Orr, P. (eds.). (2016). *Video and Filmmaking as Psychotherapy: Research and Practice*. Abingdon: Routledge.

Craig, C. (2009). *Exploring the Self Through Photography*. London and Philadelphia: Jessica Kingsley Publishers.

Craig, C. (2014). Photography in care homes: Methods for researching practice. In *Sage Research Methods Cases*. www.delloewenthal.com.

Gee, J., and Loewenthal, D. (2013). Working with despair: A phenomenological investigation. *Psychology and Psychotherapy: Theory Research and Practice*, 86: 229–243.

Gibson, N. (2018). *Therapeutic Photography: Enhancing Self-Esteem, Self-Efficacy and Resilience*. London and Philadelphia: Jessica Kingsley Publishers.

Grundtvig Lifelong Learning Programme. (2012–2014). *PhototherapyEurope in Prisons*. https://artescommunity.eu/photherapyeurope-in-prisons/.

Heron, J. (1986). *Six Category Intervention Analysis: Human Potential Research Project*. Guildford: University of Surrey.

Ingham, M. B. N., Nela Milic, N., Kantas, V., Andersdotter, S., Lowe, P. (2023). Handbook of Research on the Relationship Between Autobiographical Memory and *Photography*. *Advances in Media, Entertainment, and the Arts*. Pennsylvania: IGI Global.

Kopytin, A. (2013). Chapter 12, Photography and art therapy. In D. Loewenthal (ed.), *Phototherapy and Therapeutic Photography in a Digital Age*. Hove: Routledge.

Krauss, D. (2009). *Phototherapy and Reminiscence with the Elderly: Photo-Reminiscence*. Unpublished paper given at the 2009 International Symposium on PhotoTherapy and Therapeutic Photography, Turku, Finland, 11 June.

Loewenthal, D. (2013a). Talking pictures therapy as brief therapy in a school setting. *Journal of Creativity in Mental Health*, 8: 21–34.

Loewenthal, D. (2013b). *Phototherapy and Therapeutic Photography in a Digital Age*. Hove: Routledge.

Loewenthal, D. (2015a). The therapeutic use of photographs in the United Kingdom criminal justice system. *European Journal of Counselling and Psychotherapy*, 17(1): 39–56.

Loewenthal, D. (2015b). Evaluating the therapeutic use of photographs in European prisons. *Counselling Psychology Quarterly*, 30(1): 68–75.

Loewenthal, D. (2018). The therapeutic use of photography: Phototherapy and therapeutic photography In L. Pauwels and D. Mannay (eds.), *Sage Handbook of Visual Research Methods*, 2nd edition. London: Sage.

Martin, R. (2013). Inhabiting the image: Photography, therapy and re-enactment photography. In D. Loewenthal (ed.), *Phototherapy and Therapeutic Photography in a Digital Age*, pp. 69–81. Hove: Routledge.

www.midjourney.com/home/.

Nunez, C. (2009). The self portrait, a powerful tool for self-therapy. *European Journal of Psychotherapy and Counselling*, 11(1): 51–61.

Parella, C., and Loewenthal, D. (2013). Community phototherapy. In D. Loewenthal (ed.), *Phototherapy and Therapeutic Photography in a Digital Age*. Hove: Routledge.

Saita, E., Parrella, C., Facchin, F., and Iterlli, F. (2014). The clinical use of photography: A single case, multi-method study of the therapeutic processes. *Research in Psychotherapy, Psychopathology, Process and Outcome*, 17(1): 1–8.

Simmons, M. (2013). A creative photographic approach: Interpretation and healing through creative practice. In D. Loewenthal (ed.), *Phototherapy and Therapeutic Photography in a Digital Age*. Hove: Routledge.

Spence, J. (1986). *Putting Myself in the Picture: A Political, Personal and Photographic Autobiography*. London: Camden Press.

Stamp, R., Stephenson, S., and Loewenthal, D. (2009). *Report on the Evidence Base for Creative Therapies: A Systematic Review*. London: UKCP.

Weiser, J. (1993 [1999]). *Phototherapy Techniques: Exploring the Secrets of Personal Snapshots and Family Albums*, 2nd edition. Vancouver: Phototherapy Centre.

Index

Note: page numbers in *italics* indicate an illustration on the corresponding page.